Ms. Emily mountain!

You have a wonderful

Best wishes!

DT P_____

5/28/91

Mother always said, ". . ."

Mother always said, ". . ."

CHILDHOOD VALUE LESSONS
APPLIED TO PERSONAL
AND BUSINESS SUCCESS

by
Robert L. Popovich

Mother Always Said, ". . ." is a work of non-fiction except that
several names of persons have been changed.

Produced by Acorn Press, Lancaster, Pennsylvania
Text designed by Sutter House, Lititz, Pennsylvania

<u>To the Mothers of the World</u>

MUCH HAS BEEN WRITTEN of your contributions, but most efforts to describe them have failed to capture their essence. From cleanliness to faith, from guidance to education, from adversity to resolution, from hope to reality, and from discipline to love, you've filled every void and softened every fall. With this in mind, we hold on to what has been so dear to us but at the same time struggle to establish our independence and demonstrate that your efforts weren't in vain.

Your selfless ability to do so much for so many while denying yourself has all too often been rewarded by our taking you for granted. Although we celebrate your deeds on a national day of honor, we frequently forget that it is the small acknowledgments of appreciation that you most cherish and desire. Your trust, faith, encouragement and love serve as a constant reminder of what is truly important in life.

To all the mothers of the world from all the children of the world for all that you have done and all that is yet to come, we simply want to say,

"Thank you."

CONTENTS

INTRODUCTION

IN 1980 I WAS WORKING as a free-lance management consultant in New York City. Fresh out of the relatively secure and predictable corporate world, I eagerly looked forward to an entrepreneurial future that held seemingly limitless potential but also great uncertainty and intense competition. Even though I had had a successful corporate career, which translates into "never having been fired," I was experiencing a classic case of mixed feelings. So it's not difficult to understand my sense of urgency in wanting to move forward as quickly as possible to avoid any second thoughts about a decision that at the time seemed irreversible. During my second week of independence, I was having lunch with an old client and friend, who presented me with my first window of opportunity.

John had many contacts in private industry as well as extensive governmental contacts in Europe. He asked if I would be interested in speaking at a conference in West Germany. Without the slightest hesitation, I eagerly accepted. He went on to say that the original speaker had canceled and that the conference coordinator was desperate.

Trying to ignore the implication that they would take anyone at that point, I began asking obvious questions. For example, to whom would I be speaking? On what topic? For how long? Each question was met with the same refrain. *He had no idea.* All he could tell me was the name of the conference leader, the city, the date, and where I would be staying. All other details would be provided upon my arrival. He tried to reassure me that all would go well. And, "Oh, yes, there is one final, but critical point—you will be leaving this evening."

Under normal conditions I might have been more concerned about the topic and audience, but with little time to spare, those details would have to wait. I rushed to my apartment and packed only the essentials—my passport, a change of clothes, toothbrush, toilet paper and Berlitz phrase book.

From the airport to my arrival in Frankfurt, my mind was racing. All I could think was, "What an incredible opportunity!" I had forgotten one of Mother's more profound and critical pearls of wisdom, but it was one I would soon remember. Mother would say, "Nothing is ever as good as it seems, nor as bad as it seems."

Jetlagged but excited, I walked through one of those endless international arrival corridors, and successfully cleared customs agents whose steely eyes would compel the most innocent man to confess to crimes he had never contemplated committing. Upon exiting I looked around anxiously and spotted a gentleman holding a sign bearing my name. He looked nervous too, and it was probably our mutual anxiety that attracted us to one another. Before I could ask any questions, I found myself seated in the back of a conference courtesy car. After catching my breath, I asked the driver how long it would take to reach the conference center. He stated with evident pride, "One hour on the Autobahn; that would be two and a half hours in the United States." As soon as we exited the airport parking lot, I knew what he meant. In seconds we were cruising in excess of one-hundred miles per hour. The countryside was a beautiful blur.

As we pulled into the driveway of the conference center, I noticed a gentleman at the entrance pacing back and forth. Intense relief filled his face when he spied me seated in the passenger seat. Even before we came to a complete stop, he grabbed the door handle, he reached in and began shaking my hand, while simultaneously pulling me out of the car. "Thank goodness you're here! You go on in ten minutes." I asked nervously, "What is the general makeup of the audience?"

"High-level executives to first-line supervisors from five countries," he replied. Further questioning uncovered that the audience was *sorely* disappointed that the original speaker had fallen ill and that an unknown *substitute* would be taking his place. At that point my pulse was pumping at somewhere near the speed of light, which I could only assume was a precursor to hyperventilation. I knew I was up the proverbial creek without a paddle.

I searched my mind for a psychological life-preserver, and Mother immediately came to mind. I heard her saying, **"Robert, run to the problem. It is your greatest opportunity if you know how to take advantage of it."** My mother's words had once again come to the rescue. A feeling of calmness and confidence replaced anxiety and self-doubt.

When I was introduced, I looked into the impatient eyes of a sizable audience. I took a deep breath and began with, **"Mother always said, 'Robert, asking good questions is like eating a lot of fish. They both develop great minds.'"** Their faces began to soften. I could see they were beginning to be interested. I had found a common denominator. *Each of us has a mother, and every mother has tremendous insights to offer.* As I tried another of my mother's maxims and then introduced still another, I offered anecdotes from my youth and business career to illustrate each point. My message was that in business as in life the greatest wisdom, and the most valuable information often comes from the humblest of sources. My mother, Dorothy Popovich, a woman with little formal schooling, taught me more about how to succeed in business and as an individual than all my years of schooling and the writings of a multitude of "authorities."

The more I shared, the more they showed their appreciation. They were laughing and nodding. Our shared energy and common experiences turned the original hour into two. No one seemed to notice or care.

I was encouraged by their response but, more importantly, truly excited to have shared an experience that transformed a culturally diverse audience into a homogeneous one. At the conclusion of my presentation, many of them made it a point to stop and share some of their own "motherly" experiences. It was Mother's Day out of season, and a day that shaped the rest of my consulting career.

Over the past decade, I have found colleagues, friends and clients the world over equally delighted by my mother's maxims and stories. The encouragement of these individuals prompted me to write this book based on her philosophy and values.

In citing my own experiences as my sources, I am not claiming that my mother or I coined all these phrases. Some are original, but others are adaptations of well-known maxims from great philosophers and individuals representing many different cultures and societies. My goal is to illustrate how these messages have affected my life and to provide a source of experience that others can not only enjoy but also identify with and successfully apply. Ultimately, however, everyone must find the answers to life's questions within himself.

This book is not only dedicated to my mother, but to mothers the world over. The example of courage they set in facing life's daily challenges often goes unnoticed, but they perform their job with a zeal, intensity and dedication that would rival that showed in any profession.

To those professional women of the world who have forged new ground by taking their rightful place in every segment of business and society, I applaud you as well. Dorothy was a member of your club thirty-five years ago. And to every mother's child, I offer this personal diary of growing up with Mother, in hopes that you might revisit yours.

PROLOGUE

MY MOTHER IS THE THIRD OLDEST CHILD in a family of nine brothers and sisters. Born in 1918, she is a product of a proud Serbian-American heritage and values that committed her to a strong work ethic and devotion to family. This commitment was tested at an early age when her father died unexpectedly. Her mother asked her to drop out of school and find a job to help support the family. This was difficult for her to accept, but what she didn't know was that she was about to gain an education that would challenge and in many instances surpass most formal equivalents.

When I was twelve years old, my mother's eventual employer, surrogate father and mentor, Morris

Chamovitz, related the story of how my mother came to work for him. He said a young, innocent, beautiful and determined-looking girl entered his store one day seeking employment. He asked about her education and experience. She explained her family situation. He replied that many others were facing similar difficulties. My mother began desperately searching her mind for a tangible quality he might find attractive, and then said, "I'm also hardworking and honest!" He was still unimpressed. She realized that she would have to come up with something of greater value than the others equally needing employment had offered. As her anxiety level rose and fear of failing the family, she made her last bid for success and said, "What if I work for you free for one month, then you can tell me what I'm worth?" Shocked, but impressed, he said, "You're hired!"

After only a week, Morris' partner Harry declared that they had found a diamond in the rough. He voted for waiving the trial period and recommended offering her a salary. Morris balked, not because he didn't agree, but because he would often say, "A deal's a deal." If you give your word, you are expected to keep it. He saw this as her first lesson in business and what he sensed would be the beginning of a lifelong personal and business relationship.

Thus Mother learned an invaluable lesson, which she conveyed as follows: "Always run toward adversity, not away from it. It's your greatest opportunity if you know how to take advantage of it." When you run away, you lose something far more important than just the immediate "contest." You also lose self-respect, and this is the heaviest loss. But when you confront adversity, you gain something much more valuable than any tangible prize such as a job or money. You gain self-esteem and pride. You become a stronger, more effective person. And sometimes you gain tangible benefits as well. (Incidentally, my mother received full back pay after she was hired permanently!)

Mother always said, "..."

IMAGE

Mother always said, "Robert, . . .
. . . don't forget what your last name is;
you represent all of us, not just yourself!"

EVERY MORNING WHEN I LEFT for school or went out to play, Mother would holler before I was out of earshot, "Don't forget what your last name is; you represent all of us, not just yourself!" Certainly such messages were to some extent meant to warn me to "behave." In a staunchly religious Eastern Orthodox family, respect and good behavior topped the list of life's rules. It was understood from a very early age that breaking those rules was considered a capital offense, which meant severe verbal admonitions that bordered on inquisitions. But no matter how harsh the words, they were delivered in a lesson format that required behavioral modifications if privileges were to be restored.

Our community in Aliquippa, Pennsylvania, could certainly be considered a true melting pot of Europeans who had come to America. Serbians, Greeks, Italians, Jews, Poles and other eastern European groups had settled in this steel town in western Pennsylvania. Cleanliness, honesty, respect and hard work were the value cornerstones of all these groups.

As I approached the transitional period from boyhood to being considered a young man, I was ready one day for the usual refrain. As I went out the door on my way to school, Mother shouted, "Have a nice day, and don't forget . . ." Before she could finish, I said, "Excuse me, Mother. I know it by heart. 'Don't forget what my last name is.' Right?" Her immediate reaction was one of surprise, followed by a rather smug but approving smile. I was relieved to see that my remark was not considered disrespectful, but I asked, "Did I say something funny?" She replied, "No. I'm just pleased that it only took you thirteen years to remember!"

She went on to say that each of us is individually accountable for our actions, and also it must be remembered that each person's behavior reflects on the family and community. In small ethnic communities, news travels fast, especially bad news. Embarrassing the family is something to be avoided at all costs.

The shoe store where my mother worked had developed an excellent reputation over the years.

Although the store didn't have a written image statement, it was known for providing high-quality shoes at a reasonable price. In this it was not unlike other stores, except it stood head and shoulders above its competitors when it came to customer service and overall flexibility. That commitment translated into personalized attention, no matter how big or small the purchase was. Any complaint was met with immediate action, and when in doubt, the decision went in favor of the customer.

One day after running several errands for my mother, I returned to the store just as she was confronted by a visibly irritated customer. It was during the holiday season, and the store was bustling with frantic but friendly holiday shoppers.

As the angry customer approached the counter, my mother asked if she could be of assistance. He responded in a loud voice, "Yes! I bought these shoes here and they've fallen apart. I want a full refund!" He spoke so loudly that everyone in the store turned and looked. As Mother examined the shoes (their condition dated them as pre-World War II), she asked if he had a receipt. (I thought an etched stone tablet would have been more like it.) He didn't. She went on to ask when the shoes were purchased. He couldn't remember. The scam he was pulling had become glaringly obvious.

By this time, the other customers were watching this

exchange. I suspected they were all interested in how the situation would be handled. I was sure that every one of them would have supported my mother had she refused the man's claim.

She asked him to wait a moment while she checked with the owner. She explained the situation to Morris, and he asked what she would like to do and why. "Well," she said, "under any other conditions, I would be justified in turning him away. After all, he doesn't have a receipt, and further we don't even know if he purchased the shoes from our store. But I recommend we give him the refund anyway." When Morris asked why, she explained that the store was full of good customers, and the incident had drawn so much attention that she felt it could be taken advantage of from an "image" point of view. He agreed.

She returned to the gentleman and thanked him for waiting. "Sir, it is store policy that a customer provide a receipt, or some type of information to verify that the shoes were purchased here. I'm sure you can understand why we have such a policy, but . . ." Before she could continue, he interrupted in a rage demanding to see the owner. She said that wasn't necessary since the owner had already authorized her to give a full refund under certain conditions. The customer quieted and asked what the conditions were. She said that he would have to fill out his name, address and phone number for their records. In addition, any future refunds he might request would have to meet the store's standard policy.

He filled out the information, took the money and immediately left the store. After he was gone, my teenage mind needed to resolve why she had given him the refund. She said, "Even though there is a store policy, there were other factors involved. With the number and type of customers present, the situation became an opportunity, not a problem." I asked, "But what's going to happen now that everyone in the store saw you break the store policy? Won't they try and take advantage of you in the future?"

She said it was highly unlikely since the majority were long-standing customers. She went on to point out that by stating the requirements to the customer, it is also unlikely that he would ever come back, and if he did, he now knew that he would have to produce a valid receipt. Even more importantly, she suspected that the customers recognized that her handling of the situation was out of consideration for them more than for the benefit of the angry customer. This lesson would serve me well later in the business world.

Everything that each employee says or does contributes toward painting a portrait of the company to its customers. In fact, companies spend millions of dollars to develop a specific mindset in the marketplace. When we mention a specific name such as Coca Cola, an immediate image comes to mind, i.e., the type of product and its relative quality.

While speaking to the national sales force of a reputable lumber company, I was asked a question about a large customer that the company had lost some two years before. It seems that the customer asked for a credit of $2,000 for lumber that was returned. The sales representative handling the account said he had irrefutable evidence that the customer was wrong. The rep, who was the firm's senior account executive, turned out to be correct. The conflict eventually turned into a battle of wills between the sales representative and the customer. The outcome was that the customer refused to do business with the company ever again. In addition, the lumber company found out that the customer went on to share this "gross injustice" with anyone who would listen.

Further questioning also revealed that the customer had been one of the firm's biggest accounts. The president of the company asked what I would recommend. I related the story of my mother and the incident of the returned shoes. I stressed that it is important for every representative of the company to remember what his or her last name is, i.e., that they represent the entire company and not just themselves. I advised that, even though the sales representative was acting in the company's best interest, the best course of action would be to send the customer a total refund, with interest, accompanied by a personal cover letter from the president. I couldn't guarantee that his business would return, but at least it might serve to eliminate his negative image campaign, and from that perspective should be considered investment spending.

At that point, a break was taken and the president took me aside to discuss the situation. He wondered what effect my suggestion would have on his top performer. I said the rep might feel a temporary loss in prestige among his peers and a sense that upper management was not pleased with his handling of the situation, but I added that if a broad and objective perspective were taken that didn't indict the rep's actions, everyone would gain from the experience. The president agreed. The meeting was reconvened, and the president took the floor.

Saying that he understood that it is difficult to reconsider this type of issue, he stressed that the negative impacts far outweighed the principle at stake. He knew the president of this account personally, and he was not only influential in the industry, but also was never one to quit on an issue. In other words, it had become a religious cause, not just routine business.

The president went on to say that he would personally write a letter of apology to the customer, along with the full refund with interest. He admitted that he recognized that much time had passed, and he knew there would be little hope of regaining the account, but that was not his primary objective. If the refund only served to stop the disgruntled customer's mud- slinging campaign, it would be worth it. He went on to point out that the company's success had always been attributed to hard work, honesty and fairness to its customers. His decision was a reflection of this philosophy. The veteran sales representative nodded in agreement. And as the president started to sit down, he smiled warmly and said, *"And let's not forget what our last name is . . ."*

REVENGE

Mother always said, "Robert, . . .
. . . before setting out on revenge,
first dig two graves—one for your enemy
and one for yourself."

WHEN I WAS APPROXIMATELY TWELVE years old, we lived in a wonderful neighborhood. Our family home was set on a large and beautiful yard dotted with a variety of fruit trees. Each year we eagerly awaited the coming of fall and the annual harvest of our favorite fruit—the most delicious red and yellow apples. This fall, however, would be different. We would reap the seeds of deceit, not the wonderful fruit that we had become so accustomed to.

The problem began when our neighbor registered a complaint. It seems several of the larger trees branches hung well into her yard resulting in many apples falling on her property. We made a sincere attempt to pick them up each day, but it wasn't enough to keep her lawn apple free. The situation escalated from polite expressions of dissatisfaction to direct and hostile confrontations. Then without explanation, she stopped complaining. My parents were relieved but befuddled. Why the sudden turnaround? It wouldn't be long before the mystery would be solved.

During the height of the picking season, we could count on four bushels of apples a day, but over the next two weeks our haul was halved. We began noticing a significant absence of apples on the branches that reached into her yard and none on the ground on her side of the property line. I asked Mother, "How could she take them without asking?" Mother replied, "She probably felt justified. You see, Robert, none of us likes to feel as though he's doing anything wrong, so we rationalize. It's her way of getting back at us. She's never complained in past years, so maybe she's having difficulties in her life that have made her overly sensitive." Her explanation did not reduce my frustration.

My brother and I were angry and felt a need for some kind of revenge. We were young, and life's problems were black and white; what was right and what was wrong always seemed so obvious.

One day my parents were discussing the situation, and I felt compelled to voice my opinion. Self-righteously I blurted, "This woman is a thief and should be punished!" I was shocked when my parents showed little support for—or even reaction to—my outburst. This was an open-and-shut case as far as I was concerned. The only question that remained was what type of punishment she should receive. I voted for calling the police and sharing the news with all the neighbors.

My mother asked, "Robert, are you seeking justice or revenge? What good would it do to call the police? Even if we did, what do you think the consequences might be?" I hated when she did that. Always asking logical questions that made me think. Why couldn't it be as simple as it is on television or in the movies? The good guys totally right and the bad guys totally wrong, the good guys always winning and justice prevailing.

I responded, "I don't want revenge, I just want what is right!" Then my mother said, "Knowing the right thing to do in life isn't always as easy as it seems. And in this case, there are many other things to consider besides just making her pay for what she has done. She's been our neighbor for over twenty years. Shouldn't that count for something?" I held my ground: "Well, the least we can do is confront her with the fact that we know she is a thief." At that my father chimed in with the big kibosh,"What good would it do to tell her what she already knows?"

What my parents had that I didn't was experience in life. They knew that this woman was simply a human

13

being who had made an error in judgment. From time to time, we all make wrong decisions. And even if she thought that we would never uncover the truth, she would probably experience much greater pain from her own conscience.

It was only a matter of two weeks before she came over to talk with my mother. It was obvious she wanted to confess. Mother stopped her before she could begin. She said, "Look, Louise, I can see that you've suffered too long over this matter already. You've been a wonderful neighbor and good friend for too many years to let this one incident change all that. Let's forget it ever happened, and whenever you want apples for yourself or your family, you are always welcome to take them."

What a lady! Benevolent, you say? Even a candidate for a Nobel Peace Prize? I believe that compassion *is* Mother's basic nature, but her motives went much deeper. Her values and experience had taught her that forgiveness is more practical than revenge. Although it took quite some time for our relationship with the neighbor to return to normal, it eventually did. In fact, it ultimately became much stronger and more meaningful. It wasn't until years later that I would revisit this lesson in a setting designed to uphold justice, but transformed into a self-serving and vindictive situation that almost ruined two legal careers and a respected law firm.

Based in Washington, D.C., the firm was experiencing the negative effects of increased competition from an ever-increasing number of firms entering the market. The firm in question was realizing that they needed some form of a marketing plan. Since marketing is basically new to the legal profession, I faced inherent barriers not least of which was the perception that the term *marketing* is a euphemism for that unspeakable term: *selling*. Marketing is considered the antithesis of what the profession represents to the public and its own self-image. I understood and sympathized with this concern. Further complicating matters was the fact that the firm suffered from the kind of rivalries between departments and among individuals that exist in every organization. It wasn't until I had been consulting with the firm for a while, however, that I was to become a witness to an extreme example in which a personal rivalry between two of the stronger personalities in the firm turned into open warfare.

On one side was a senior litigator who was successful and highly respected by the public and by his peers. In his personality, though, he showed little patience for anyone who questioned his ideas or methods of practice. He was totally consumed by his work and did not believe in delegating responsibilities. On the other hand, his rival was a young, bright, aggressive attorney who was considered a maverick by his adversary. The younger man's approach was one of team playing, actively shared participation and significant delegation. Their different personalities and management styles set up a situation in which both parties were unwilling to deal with the facts.

During my engagement I witnessed a growing and overt animosity between the two attorneys. The major source of irritation was the criteria that were used for determining voting rights and percentage of profit-sharing for partners. The senior attorney argued that rights and shares should be directly related to tenure, while the junior member felt that an individual's contribution to the firm's profits should also be a major consideration. Their perceptions seemed to be mutually exclusive.

Partnership meetings became the occasion for constant personal attacks. The other partners and associates went from being innocent bystanders to taking sides. The situation became a war of age versus youth. As the weeks passed, the office became a virtual battleground for the two factions, each proclaiming victories in the daily skirmishes, while the basic fiber of the firm slowly, but consistently deteriorated.

I couldn't help but think of Mother's question about revenge during the apple incident.

During my daily activities at the firm, I would meet frequently with various departments and individuals. I was fortunate to have built a positive relationship with the younger attorney, revolving around the business plan and strategies for marketing the firm. As time passed, however, I felt it was appropriate to begin some form of constructive dialogue with him about the personal conflict. After several weeks of general discussions, we began to analyze the basic causes. I asked what he thought was the root of the problem. He said, "He's one religion, and I'm another."

I asked whether he had given any thought to the ramifications of this ongoing battle. He paused for a long time and said, "It's been devastating, not only personally, but equally from the firm's point of view." But he said that he knew that his cause was just and that the junior members of the firm would eventually wear down the senior partners. I asked, "But at what price?" He replied with tongue in cheek sarcasm, "I can see by the look on your face that you're going to give me one of your mother's stories."

We went over the case of the missing apples. This was followed by a detailed analysis of the current problem that involved his taking himself out of the situation and adopting an objective, third-party point of view. We began by discussing the major factors affecting the situation and then labeling each of them as controllable, uncontrollable, positive, negative and neutral. The next step was to list all the inherent obstacles he was facing and then specific options and action steps. After a lengthy analysis, he agreed that the best strategy was for him to accept the situation as it was, and not as he perceived or thought it should be. Next he agreed to stop all direct or indirect confrontations that weren't case-related, and to show a greater degree of respect and cooperation. He also agreed to disband his group of loyal followers and advise them as to why.

Over the next two months tensions began to drop dramatically. Even his adversary noticed. I asked the senior attorney how this affected his perceptions and thoughts about the problem. He replied that it had given him a lot to think about. For him to make such a statement can be considered the equivalent of a religious conversion. As time passed, the two men were able to develop at least a manageable working relationship and a degree of mutual respect.

My engagement with the firm had ended and I was packing up to leave when the young attorney stopped by my office. I told him I was proud of the manner in which he had handled the situation. He thanked me but said it was motivated more from a practical point of view than a personal one. I asked what he meant. "Well, I know I'll never have any real relationship with him, but that isn't what's important. If we had kept going on in this manner, it would have meant the demise of the firm." I nodded. It wasn't an ideal situation, but it worked. The focus of the individuals and firm slowly but surely returned to their original purpose: the art of practicing law, and not revenge.

FIRST IMPRESSIONS

Mother always said, "Robert, . . .
*. . . first impressions are like the first few
steps in a race — they can give you an early
lead, but the race isn't over until you
cross the finish line!"*

IT WAS MY FIRST DATE. Boy, was I nervous. Just
think, I was going out with one of the brightest, prettiest
and most sought-after girls in my class; Carol Mancini—
cheerleader.

I was newly licensed, spit-shined and ready to go, but
first I had to pass Mother's hygiene inspection: "Did you
bathe, brush your teeth and shine your shoes?"
Affirmative on all counts. "What about your
underwear—are they clean in case you're in an accident
and have to go to the hospital? I won't have my son
caught dead in dirty underwear!" Then the critical
instructions in manners: "Remember to be polite and
talk clearly when you introduce yourself to her parents.
Nobody likes a weak-kneed boy, especially a girl. And
most of all, show respect at all times. Bring her home on

time and if you have any trouble call us, no matter what time it is. Remember . . . etc., etc., etc." I was exhausted; it almost wasn't worth the date.

Mother's inquisition was so draining it left little strength for becoming nervous. Before long, I found myself pulling up in front of Carol's house. I parked the car and took a deep breath. As I walked up the steps, I could hear a loud thumping sound that reminded me of a bass drum. It was coming from underneath my sports jacket. I thought, this is why they call it a heart throb. I rang the doorbell and was met by an older lady I assumed was Carol's grandmother.

As I entered the living room, I was greeted by Carol's parents and numerous religious articles prominently displayed on every table and adorning every wall. I introduced myself and shook hands with everyone. I almost felt compelled to declare I had been an altar boy for over ten years, but Mother's parting advice still echoed in my ears: "There are three things you never discuss: politics, family and religion, especially on the first date." I was offered a seat and soft drink while I waited for Carol who was still getting ready. This was my first date and I had not yet learned that this is standard procedure, even when the date is made a week in advance. Undaunted, I willingly waited.

Her parents began the conversation. It reminded me of a little snow ball that slowly starts rolling down a hill and eventually grows into an avalanche. It went something like this: "How long has your family been in the area?" *Since my birth and we plan on living here forever.* "How many brothers and sisters do you have?" *I have one older brother who is the president of his class.* "Are your parents still living?" *Yes, and they said to tell you hello.* "What does your father do for a living?" *He doesn't. He's in the hospital with tuberculosis, but my mother has a job! She's been quite successful.* The grandmother compassionately chimed in with, "I'll light a candle for your father." I thanked her and then told them that I respected Carol very much and that I had never received a speeding ticket or had an accident while driving. They smiled approvingly.

Just as I began to feel a little comfortable, I noticed the grandmother looked concerned. She appeared preoccupied and equally troubled. Still on my best behavior, I asked if something was wrong. She said no, except for wondering why I was so skinny. I told her it was hereditary. She offered to feed me some bone-sticking pasta and added that she was concerned that my slight build would not be conducive for working in the fields. I thanked her and said I had never thought of it that way. Her parents smiled and explained that her offer was Grandmother's way of telling someone she liked them. I was elated.

Mother always said, If you don't impress the

23

grandparents and parents, it's not likely you're going to impress the girl. She was right. After almost an hour, Carol finally appeared. It was worth the wait; she looked absolutely stunning. Apologizing for being late, she asked if I'd had a chance to talk with her parents. Since my back was to our elders, I nodded and rolled my eyes.

We had survived the inquisitions and we went on to survive the evening and traffic.

The next day I ran into Carol at school. She said that not only had she had fun, but I was a hit with her family.

Love bloomed eternal over the next year. As we approached our first anniversary, I was prompted to ask a question that had long been on my list of things to discover before I departed this Earth: "Why did she take so long to get ready on our first date?" She was noticeably embarrassed, but willing to share the answer: "Well . . . it's like this. My parents tell me to be intentionally late so they can have a chance to talk to the boy." I laughed and said we could have saved an hour. She asked how. "Well, they could have joined in my mother's pre-departure interview."

Mother always placed a great deal of emphasis on making a positive first impression. Her definition of this went beyond the traditional factors of dress, attitude and manner. She saw first impressions as a reflection of a person's total character, experience, beliefs and interests. The first impression sets the tone for what follows, and if the first impression is phoney, then the true character will naturally surface. In others words, people eventually "get caught in the act of being themselves."

Whether consulting to government or industry, I recognized why Mother gave positive impressions such a high importance. She stressed that preparation was truly the key. If you knew who your audience was and prepared accordingly, the odds would be in your favor.

One day I was about to test these early lessons in one of the most challenging situations I have ever faced. I was representing one of my New York City clients who had engaged me to call on a potential customer my client had been trying to gain business from for many years. I never imagined in my wildest dreams that I would feel like I was on the set of one of my favorite movies, *Casablanca*.

I began my research by analyzing the basic data of the targeted company, i.e., products, markets and major competitors. Additionally, I did extensive investigation into the nationality and cultural orientation of its owner. I interviewed other suppliers who had done business with him in the past to gain more personal insights. The hard data were relatively straightforward.

Company: Fifth largest supplier of textile goods in the world. Little or no debt, and an impeccable reputation for tough but fair negotiating tactics. Highly respected in the industry and substantial contributor to Middle Eastern health organizations, i.e., Armenian hospitals and ethnic universities.

President and Sole Proprietor: Considered one of the most inscrutable but honorable men in the industry. Very religious. Relatively impossible to gain an appointment with and never discusses his personal interests or business intentions. Five sons, all Harvard graduates. Each son holds a key position in the company. Style direct and to the point. Very time- and value-conscious.

It would be several months before an appointment could be arranged. Gaining access required calling in a series of "markers" and, equally important, trading on the excellent reputation of the company I was representing. When I finally received the call that the president would see me, I began trying to envision the man, and what type of impression I would make on him. I had no set plan, other than to practice the basic principles I had been taught from an early age: common courtesy and respect. No more, no less.

As I entered his offices on Park Avenue and presented myself to the receptionist, I noticed that the interior decorator had selected a modern decor colored with a strong Middle Eastern influence. I had plenty of time to study it while I waited to be announced. I waited for two hours. Perhaps it was a test of my patience, but I was committed to stay.

When I finally entered his office, he remained seated behind a large mahogany desk completely bare except for a glass clock. The furniture was elegantly simple. Fine art from three distinctively different cultures—Russian, African and Middle Eastern—hung on the walls. Overhead was a whirling fan right out of *Casablanca*.

His imposing frame easily filled every inch of a finely woven white linen suit. He sat motionless, save for entwining a string of worry beads in a serpentine fashion between the fingers of his right hand. I stood waiting for some form of acknowledgment of my presence. None was forthcoming. The next sixty seconds turned into an emotional millennium.

He stared into my eyes and finally said in a low, raspy voice, "Why do you continue to stand, Mr. Popovich?" I replied in a soft but firm tone, "Because, sir, you haven't given me permission to be seated." In an approving tone he said, "That's right." I remained standing.

He proceeded to give a brief appraisal of my nationality, "You are Serbian?" I nodded. "They are hardworking people . . . stress honor, respect and education." I thought, "Thank God!" He then began asking questions about the history of Yugoslavia and my heritage. Fortunately, knowing the answers had been a prerequisite to maintaining membership in good standing in my family. He gestured for me to be seated. *First test passed.*

The second was determining my general awareness of world politics, and specifically the Middle East. I had worked for many years in both Europe and the Middle East representing businesses and governmental agencies. As he questioned me, I offered my assessment of the political, social and economic factors affecting the textile market. He neither denied nor confirmed my judgments.

He then asked a totally unexpected question, one that demanded ultimate diplomacy and tact. He said, "So, Mr. Popovich, who do you think is the villain in the Middle Eastern conflict?" I was caught totally by surprise, and I'm sure that was his intent. I thought, What would Mother say in this situation? Time was of the essence, but fortunately I remembered that she would often say, If you ask a better question than was asked of you, then you've given an acceptable answer. I must have paused for more than a minute, but our eyes remained locked. Trying to couch my words in the most deliberate and objective manner possible, I said, "From whose perspective, and to what end?" The response generated a small, but approving smile. *Second test passed.*

He rewarded me by offering to introduce his sons. I felt honored.

He first summoned the eldest, the heir apparent. The father said with gleaming pride, "This is my oldest son, the soon to be president of the company." After brief chitchat, the heir apparent was ordered to bring us coffee. Enter the second son. We shook hands and he was summarily dismissed to assist his older brother. The father apologized for the absence of the number three and four sons; they were on a business trip. And the whereabouts of the youngest son? "He must first serve his apprenticeship before being permitted to participate in the activities of his older brothers."

Although I tried not to project any overt interest in his treatment of his sons, he seemed to sense my curiosity. He asked, "So, what are your impressions of my sons?" I paused and then said, "I find them polite and respectful. I'm certain they represent you and the company in an honorable and competent manner." His immediate smile was almost instantly transformed into an intense expression of concern. He said, "You know, Robert, humility is not genetic; it must be taught." I agreed. *Lesson understood; third test passed.*

At this point, I was feeling quite comfortable, but emotionally exhausted. This was the moment when he finally ventured into the topic at hand. "So, what can you tell me about my business that I don't already know?" I replied, "That would be difficult to say until I have had an opportunity to find out what you perceive your strengths and needs to be. Based upon that information, I would then be in a better position to assess what, if anything, we might be able to offer you." He agreed. *Fourth test passed, with the finish line coming into sight!*

Once the finish line is crossed, Mother would say, a new race is just beginning. Those who think they have ultimately arrived fall victim to complacency and self-satisfaction. She said to never forget that we are only as good as our last performance, and each new day we are back on the track entering a new race in hopes of making another such positive impression. One of her favorite lines was, "I've paid you for yesterday, now what are you going to do for yourself and me today?" Her final point was: First impressions are only lasting impressions if we remember to treat each subsequent impression as the first.

PLANNING

Mother always said, "Robert, . . .
*. . . if you don't know where you're going,
then how can you possibly know when
you've arrived?"*

Mother was a fanatic on planning. Everything she did had a specific objective and a plan of action. No matter how small or large the task, she knew exactly what she wanted to achieve and how. One day I was sitting on our back porch looking rather forlorn. Mother asked what was wrong. I said nothing, which always meant something. After the typical coaxing, I finally shared my frustration. I was losing money on my paper route and couldn't figure out why.

I had inherited the route from a good friend who moved to Ohio. It was wonderful. He developed the route into seventy-five long-time, steady-paying customers. All I had to do was deliver the papers and collect the incredible sum of twenty dollars (clear!)

every two weeks. It would vary occasionally, but I could always count on approximately that amount. Then for some inexplicable reason my profit started dropping—from twenty dollars to seventeen and then down to the unspeakable sum of twelve dollars. I was devastated. I could see the headlines, "Paper Route Carrier Files for Bankruptcy."

Mother started asking some basic and logical questions. She said, "Have you lost any customers recently?" I said, "Yes, but only a couple." The "two" turned out to be ten, and they had not only subscribed to the daily but also the weekend edition. They were all victims of corporate relocation. Those ten represented a loss in net income of five dollars. But that still didn't explain the additional three-dollar loss. It turned out that the remainder was attributable to twelve customers who had received a special introductory subscription rate.

Mother then asked, "What's your plan for dealing with this situation?" My objectivity was so clouded with self-pity I felt I had only one choice, "I'll give up my route! It's only going to get worse, so I might as well quit right now!" She said, "Nonsense. You're not going to quit. You're going to make a plan." I gave her my squinty-eyed (*you've-got-to-be-kidding*) look, and said, "Mother, I'm only a twelve-year-old kid. I'm not a business person." She countered with her raised eyebrows (*if you think, young man, that you're going to just walk away from this job without giving it a chance, you're badly mistaken*). Aloud, she said, "You're not a businessman. Then what are you?" She went on to say that every business has a product, price and customers. My paper route was just as much a business as any other business. O.K. , maybe so, but what can a little kid do to fix the problem? She said I needed to understand why I was losing customers and what I needed to do to fix it. In other words, I needed a plan.

"Look," she said, "in one month those special introductory rates will return to their normal subscription rate and you'll get back three dollars when that happens." Then I needed to figure out where I could gain the additional five dollars, and maybe more. Excitedly I asked, "More?" She answered, "Yes. You have two ways to make more money. First, you need to ask all the daily customers if they'd be interested in subscribing to the weekend paper." (*She was right. I had never thought to ask if they'd be interested in the weekend edition. I had not stopped to think that needs and interests change. I had just assumed they'd want the same order for the rest of their lives.*)

Secondly, she said, I needed to find out whether any new families had moved into the neighborhood. Now I was getting into the spirit. I told her about a new housing development going up nearby. Many new families would be moving in over the next six months. In fact, I knew of three new kids in my class who were already living there. Their families represented a whole new set of potential customers. Boy, was I getting excited! "Thanks!" I shouted. I thought the meeting was over, but it wasn't.

Mother stopped me. "Now that you've fixed your immediate problem, what about the future?" I didn't understand what she meant, so she added, "Don't you want to avoid this problem for good? Wouldn't you like to have a plan to ensure your paper route is going to *keep* growing?" I shrugged, "Sure. But how?" She said I needed to list all my present customers and check to see whether they were happy with my delivery service and whether they had any special requests. I said, "That makes sense." She then said business is more or less based upon common-sense. If I would just remember what happened in the past, keep checking on the present and then take note of possible future events, I'd always be in pretty good shape. Her suggestion was the neatest. She said, "You know, customers always appreciate a good job, but they're even happier when you give them more than what is expected." She suggested placing the papers in their mail-boxes, especially during bad weather, instead of leaving them on their sidewalks. This was only one suggestion; she knew I could think of more.

Boy, was this great. I went from total despair to total happiness. It just took someone who wasn't emotionally involved to bring everything into focus by analyzing what was happening and why, and then develop a plan based on those answers. I was envisioning a much different headline, "Paper Route Carrier Has Record-breaking Year!"

Years later, I had an opportunity to assist an organization that specialized in cures, but found itself desperately in need of one. It was a hospital, and it was suffering from a severe case of market blues.

It was 1985 and I had the opportunity to work with a well-respected but financially troubled rehabilitation hospital in the Southwest. It was an interesting case. The hospital had an excellent staff, facility and reputation, but their admissions were amazingly low—a market location somewhere between the Rio Grande and Extinction. During one of my interviews with the hospital administrator, I asked him how bad business was, and he said, "Robert, . . . if I could just get up to 'broke,' I'd quit." I shook my head "Hmmm!" I said, "That sounds pretty bad all right." With urgency in his voice, he said, "Look . . . if we don't turn this thing around in the next three months, we'll all be looking for work. So even though I don't really think you'll make a difference, I thought we'd give it one last shot."

With that vote of confidence, I suspected that I'd be

registered to stay at the Last Resort Motor Lodge. I said, "Well . . . in this case, I hope I don't live up to your expectations." I began studying the symptoms and looking for the causes. In this case, it didn't take long to determine that the hospital had a common but acute marketing malady—no specific marketing plan.

The hospital had flourished in an era in which demand exceeded supply. The administrators had never needed a plan until rising medical costs resulted in governmental legislation to control expenditures. The outcome was stiffer competition and a more educated and selective consumer. The staff needed to analyze all these factors and more.

My research uncovered the following: 1. the public perceived the hospital as primarily a research center and not as the excellent in-patient care facility it had matured into, 2. none of the existing clients really knew what the hospital's total service capabilities were, 3. the hospital had no marketing department, and 4. the staff had no specific plan for marketing the hospital's services. All of its business was based on direct referrals.

After the findings were reviewed and confirmed, a marketing plan was developed. It outlined short- and long-term objectives and strategies for dealing with the identified internal and external issues. My role was to provide the structure for the establishment of the marketing effort and to assist in the development of strategy. The medical staff, administration and board members worked tirelessly to develop the plan and implement it, made the necessary sacrifice of long hours and commitment to turn the plan into reality. It was a wonderful example of a quality product being supported by a motivated staff. After several months, the rate of admissions began to increase. In addition, the hospital's new image started to take hold in the market. The administration, staff and hospital board were very pleased with the results. My job was done.

Before leaving the hospital for the last time, I stopped in to bid farewell to the administrator. We briefly discussed the plan and its potential. He said, "When you're too close to an issue, it's difficult to keep things in proper focus." I nodded in agreement. He continued, "At times, gaining a fresh and different perspective can really make the difference. You know, we had all the ingredients; we just needed the recipe. It was a case of identifying the real illness, rather than randomly treating symptoms." In this instance, the right prescription turned out to be a marketing plan. My parting comment was, "Thank you for the opportunity and hope to see you soon." He walked me to the door, and said, " You can *plan* on it."

Planning, Mother would say, can play a positive role in every aspect of our lives, not just in business. Whether your considering a trip, career, relationship or an event, planning can save valuable time, money and unnecessary frustration. The key, she would say, is to start with a specific objective that is both realistic and at the same time, challenging. The reason for most failures in life, she'd remark, is more often poor planning than incompetence or inadequate resources. And her final point was to expect the unexpected and never lose sight of your original goal. It may take some time, but one thing is certain, you'll always know when you've arrived.

CURIOSITY

Mother always said, "Robert, . . .
. . . the only thing that is more predictable than the need to eat, is the need to discover."

Every summer I would visit my maternal grandmother for two weeks. Each morning began with pancakes to order, at midday there was homemade ice cream, and never was there a bedtime curfew. Coupled with the numerous friends I had made over previous summers, it would have been difficult for a ten-year old to ask for more.

One of our favorite games was playing stickball. The rules were similar to baseball, but the equipment was makeshift—a tennis ball and a broomstick. And our diamond was the street, which was lined with parked cars, rowhouses, and yards neatly cordoned off with fences. The owners' pride in their homes and flower gardens was obvious.

39

But there was one—a large Victorian-style home that belonged to a recluse—from which we stayed away. It was located at the far end of the street, and the window blinds were always drawn. The only signs of life were the cats perched on every window between the blinds and the glass. The owner was frightening—gnarled hands, scraggly beard, toothless mouth and the same ragged clothes he never changed. Each of us had his own theory about his past and how he'd come to be so peculiar, but none of us really knew why. No one even knew his name. My grandmother and mother both cautioned me to leave him alone.

His was the only part of the street usually free of parked cars. The only time he'd appear was when anything entered his property—namely, tennis balls, from children playing in the street. If an errant ball made its way into his yard, he would spring into action. His pattern was always the same. He would thrust open the door, run down the steps, snatch the ball, stare menacingly at the guilty parties, and then quickly disappear inside. The next day, the ball was usually found in the middle of the street cut into little pieces. The rule of the neighborhood was to never hit the ball into Mr. No Name's yard, but if you did, never make an attempt to retrieve it.

One particular day, my friend Tommy and I were playing stickball and as luck would have it, the ball found its way into the out-of-bounds yard. When Mr. No Name failed to appear on schedule, I suggested we retrieve the ball. Tommy voiced his apprehension: "Are you nuts!" My relentless badgering failed to change his mind until I resorted to the ultimate challenge. *I double-dog dared him.*

Our strategy was to enter the yard by climbing a fence that bordered the garage and was hidden from the house. We crept alongside the garage wall until we reached the ball. Exhilarated at our victory, we decided to take the opportunity to peek inside the garage. Raising ourselves slowly to a window, we peered inside. A chill went up my spine. On the far wall was a row of knives neatly aligned and ordered from the smallest up to butcher knives. Hypnotized now, we raised up higher. Below the knives was a row of machetes, also perfectly lined up. Momentarily frozen, only our eyes moved as we looked at each other in disbelief and terror. Returning to the windowpane, we raised ourselves totally upright. Our last discovery was a row of axes leaning against the wall beneath the knives and machetes. What was pounding through my head—and probably through Tommy's—was the thought, What does Mr. No Name cut up besides tennis balls?

At that point—I still can't imagine why, except that he was gripped by curiosity—Tommy suggested we take a look in the window of the house. I didn't think it was such a good idea, but he was undeterred. He resorted to my familiar tactics and said, "*I triple-dog dare you!*" Backing down from a *triple-dog dare* would most certainly ensure a permanent place in the Children's Hall of Shame. We crept forward.

Staying low, every antenna out, we were like African gazelles drinking at watering holes frequented by predators. I was holding my breath and not even aware of it.

We reached a kitchen window at the rear of the house. On tiptoe, we looked inside. At that very moment, I felt a vice-like hand grip my shoulder. Out of the corner of my eye, I saw the other hand clamp down on Tommy. A deep and scratchy voice growled, "What are you kids doing in my yard?" We both screamed. In a total state of panic, we ripped ourselves free and ran toward the fence. It was about three feet high. On the way in, we'd had to scale it, but now we took it like Jesse Owens clearing the hurdles at the Berlin Olympic Games.

I spent a restless night hiding underneath the covers, terrifying myself with fears that Mr. No Name would come after me. Fortunately, Mother was due the next morning to collect me and my things. She immediately noticed an unusual urgency on my part regarding our departure. Her relentless questioning eventually led to the truth and a severe reprimand. Her initial inclination was to demand that I go and apologize, but she eventually reversed her decision. Sensing my remorse, she stated with firmness, "All right, you don't have to apologize. But remember, it's O.K. to be curious but not if there are signs warning against it." I could not have agreed more.

Years later, I would be confronted with a similar situation, but this time the roles would be reversed. One of my fellow co-workers who was basically a good sort had an insatiable and officious curiosity. In other words, he suffered from a terminal case of the professional "Nosy Nelly" syndrome.

His behavior was analogous to that of chickens searching for food in a yard. Their heads jerk and bob in all directions, looking for anything and everything, but not quite sure exactly what. Jerry, our chicken, would enter my office saying, "Hi, Robert. What's up?" All the while his eyes were focused on my desk looking for free information. And on occasion when I had stepped out for a few moments, I would return to find him reading papers on my desk. His excuses ranged from having forgotten a report to looking for a piece of scratch paper to write a note. Finally, one day I had had enough. It had to end. Confronting him wouldn't have served any constructive purpose. My first step was to develop an objective as to what I wanted to achieve, and in this case it came in the form of a question: "How can I stop this behavior without causing ill feelings?" It would be a worthwhile challenge.

Jerry came by on one of his typical reconnaissance missions. He was totally unaware of the land mine he would face. I slowly and rather surreptitiously began moving my hand toward a targeted piece of paper. His eyes followed as if magnetically attached. It was "The Ipcress File" all over again. His sights were locked in on the target. Trying to sound nervous, I said, "Oh! Ahhh . . . did you know that the company picnic has been changed to another date?" Simultaneously, I turned the memo over to cover its contents. He began salivating. I then ignored the paper and continued the conversation. He had taken the bait. At this point I said that I had to go down the hall, and asked if he would listen for my telephone and take any messages. His reaction? "Yes, Yes! Stay as long as you like!"

I left the room, knowing full well that as soon as I left it would only be moments before he would reel in the day's prize. What he didn't know was that the catch was actually a bomb. On the other side of the paper I had typed in large bold letters, "GOTCHA!"

I returned after several minutes and thanked him for watching the phone. His expression was a mixture of embarrassment and disappointment. I asked if I'd had any messages, and he replied in an innocent and polite tone, "No," and then added, "Well . . . I'd better be going."

He didn't return for several days. When he did, we exchanged the usual amenities, until he said, "Remember the other day when you asked me to watch your phone for you?" My heart stopped. I said, "Yes?" I went through the usual self-incriminating doubts over what I had done. Then with a rather impish little-boy smirk, he said, "I guess you got me hook, line and sinker." We both looked at each other and began laughing hysterically.

And in case you're curious, the snooping ended, and we began uncovering a whole new dimension in our relationship.

ANXIETY

Mother always said, "Robert, . . .
. . . nothing is ever as good as it seems,
nor as bad as it seems, so relax and deal
with life's challenges one step at a time."

ANXIETY IS PART OF OUR MINDS from birth until we depart this world, yet this uneasiness is generally detached from objective facts. For example, whenever my mother would say the following, "Robert, we need to have a little talk," I would instinctively respond with, "Why? Did I do something wrong?" My reaction was attributable to similar requests in the past that usually meant a serious discussion was at hand. Her advice about that assumption was, even if it is a generally negative situation, don't put yourself at a disadvantage before you have all the facts. Wait and see how things develop, and then go from there. Sound and logical advice, but difficult to follow.

The definitive youthful example of high anxiety

occurs when the school principal summons a child to the office. It seems like only yesterday when I was in my sixth-grade math class and heard an ominous knock at the classroom door. A messenger handed the teacher a slip of paper with a name on it. How did we know it contained a name? Because we heard the teacher say, "I'll get him for you." Our class was equally divided—fifteen boys and fifteen girls. With that key word "him," the girls were immediately off the hook. The boys in the meantime were practicing that age-old art of appearing indifferent by looking casually out the window, while actually reviewing in their minds all recently notable misconduct and probable punishments. The teacher slowly walked center stage and said, "Robert, you are wanted in the principal's office." My immediate reaction was that someone had either passed away in the family or that I was in serious trouble.

I glanced around the room for signs of support, but was greeted with blank stares or averted eyes. This was followed by a sotto voce discussion of the likely crime and possible punishment. I tried to get up, but couldn't. I was experiencing mental and bodily dysfunction caused by acute paranoia.

As I entered the principal's domain, the secretary turned and said, "Yes. May I help you, young man?" Nearly speechless, I managed to communicate that I had been summoned. She offered me a seat.

Five minutes passed during which I was sure my heart stopped beating several times, even though I was convinced that I hadn't done anything wrong.

When I finally entered the inner office, the principal immediately stood up and came around his desk to greet me. His friendly smile and hand on my shoulder immediately began reducing my anxiety. He asked if I knew why he wanted to see me? I said I had no idea. He explained that it was about Christmas, that is, our Eastern Orthodox Christmas. He knew that we celebrated on January 7th, and he wanted to extend holiday greetings to me and my family. I thanked him and, as I turned to leave, politely suggested that in the future he consider using Western Union. He laughed.

As soon as I arrived home that day, I shared the experience with my mother. She smiled but said, "So, what did you learn from this ordeal?" I quipped, "To carry a bottle of Pepto Bismol in my lunch bag." She frowned and said that's not what she'd meant. I began laughing and told her I hadn't forgotten about waiting until all the facts are in before making judgments. She acknowledged that it's easier said than done, but if consistently practiced can serve to reduce stress and apprehension. My reaction had been a classic example of self-induced anxiety.

Some years later, I was to experience another form of high anxiety, one that was externally produced. I would be confronted with a potential loss of not only my personal freedom, but possibly something much worse.

It was 1973 and I was on my way to the Middle East to attend a conference in Kabul, Afghanistan. Never having been there before, I was eagerly looking forward to encountering a unique and fascinating culture. It was a time, however, when many countries were torn by strife between religious fundamentalists and their governments. As a student of history and languages, I couldn't have been more excited, but for some inexplicable reason I felt uneasy.

The flight was interminably long and tiring. From New York our first stop was London. We then hopped our way across Europe to Rome, our last refueling stop. As we took off again, the gentleman seated next to me struck up a conversation. He turned out to be the Indian Ambassador to the United Nations. The time passed agreeably to our next stops, Istanbul, Turkey, and then Beirut, Lebanon. After several hours, we proceeded southeast toward Tehran, Iran, or more commonly known in history as Persia. All seemed normal until the Pan Am captain came on the public address system and made an announcement that was intended to reduce fear, but in reality only served to increase it.

As the captain spoke, we were making our final approach, and I peered out my window. Dark clouds of smoke were rising around the perimeter of the airport.

The captain advised us that a separatist group was attacking government-controlled facilities, including the airport we were approaching. The captain continued, saying that he would not be permitted to park our aircraft at the assigned gate. We were to stay at the end of the runway and wait to board buses escorted by armed guards. My excitement over this trip popped like a balloon.

Before we were allowed to disembark, the guards collected all passports. No explanations were given or questions entertained. We were quickly herded onto waiting buses and driven toward an isolated hangar away from the primary target areas. The temperature outside was over 120 degrees and felt twice as hot once we entered the Quonset hut.

The guards asked everyone the same two questions: final destination and purpose of the trip. The slight comfort of being crowded together quickly dissipated as all the other passengers were released, except for me. The guards asked for my visa. I told them it was to have been wired from the United States. Not only hadn't it arrived, but the guards expressed some additional concerns. The unusually high number of custom stamps in my passport created a natural curiosity, and my being American only added to their growing suspicion. Their limited ability to speak English or any other major European language made the situation even worse. I kept telling myself to relax until all the facts were known. It was easier said than done.

The next four hours were spent in an interrogation room. Eventually an officer who spoke a modest amount of English was located. Displaying limited interest or concern, he asked the same questions over and over. I kept repeating the same responses. My anxiety began turning into quiet anger. I repeatedly asked to speak with the U.S. Consulate. The request was never acknowledged. It was as though I had never asked.

With no explanation provided, I was ordered not to leave Iran until my story was verified. Three armed guards escorted me to a waiting military vehicle. I was taken to a hotel and ordered to stay in my room. My passport and all my personal belongings, except for toiletries, were taken, and two men kept me under constant surveillance. I received no communications or explanations for the next several days. I was not allowed to make any phone calls. I kept reminding myself of Mother's "it is never as bad at it seems," since I knew that any inquiry would surely absolve me of being an actual or potential threat.

On the morning of the fourth day, I was taken to a government house for further questioning. They returned my passport and personal belongings, along with explicit instructions to leave the country and never return. I immediately boarded the next flight for Kabul.

It wasn't until the following day that the true seriousness of the incident registered. It was much like the delayed trauma accident victims sometimes experience. What came to mind was how little control we have over many events in our lives, and that we must be mentally prepared to deal with them.

Anxiety can be created by ourselves or by others. In either case, it's the mental attitude we bring to a situation that can greatly influence the outcome. Even when things appear hopeless, we need to maintain control over our senses and deal with challenges one step at a time. To do otherwise can place us in an undesirable position or at a needless disadvantage. As Mother always said, *"Nothing is ever as . . ."*

JEALOUSY

Mother always said, "Robert, . . .
. . . take your enemy and turn him into an ally.
You will then never have a greater ally."

It WAS THE HOLIDAY SEASON and Mother announced the date for our annual Christmas excursion into the city. This meant enjoying decorated department store windows and shopping for family gifts, but it also meant new holiday outfits for my brother, Charles, and myself. Older and taller, Charles would understandably receive more clothes since I could inherit some of his hand-me-downs. Mother always bought quality, but that wasn't the point. My brother's taste in clothes and any preferences were as different as our personalities. I was almost thirteen and beginning to experience my first conscious pangs of self-pity and jealousy. Sensing my distress, Mother asked, "What's wrong? You're usually very excited about our trip to the city."

With my head hanging down and eyes staring at a meaningless spot on the floor, I responded, "I guess I'm just growing up." Unconvinced, but cautious, Mother did not press the issue. She would often say that timing generally determines the outcome of a battle. In this case she chose to delay the eventual confrontation. This battle would be fought as all others were—at a later time and on neutral ground.

I went to my room and began dwelling on one of my favorite themes—the gross injustice of being the youngest sibling. My brother's accomplishments were meteoric. He was an honors student, student council representative and officer, band member and one of the most glib, quick-witted and popular members of his class. As if those attributes and accomplishments weren't enough, he was also a good athlete. What's more, the most frustrating thing was that people frequently called me by his name. I was a victim of a double whammy—always a half-step behind his accomplishments and little or no identity of my own. Whenever I would occasionally surpass one of his public records, it was treated as expected; if I fell short, it was clear I hadn't lived up to expectations. Worst of all—in a way—was the fact that my brother couldn't have been more supportive or caring. Mother Nature had seemingly dealt me a losing hand.

Later that evening, Mother came to my room and sat

down beside me on my bed. She said in her usual soft and caring voice, "So, what seems to be troubling you?" Mustering all of my strength to hide my true feelings, I proclaimed, "Nothing!" She didn't respond. She just sat quietly and waited. It wasn't long before the frustration that was overwhelming me could no longer be contained, "It's so unfair being the youngest in the family," I exclaimed, "especially when your brother is so much better than you at everything." Instead of a litany of reasons why I shouldn't feel that way, she said, "You know that I was the third oldest child in my family of nine. Can you imagine what *that* was like—I mean, mornings were a circus. Nine children trying to get ready for the day, and each of them wanting special attention from your grandparents." She was beginning to draw me out of my mood. I said, "That must have been wild." She laughed and agreed: "It was, but somehow it all seemed to work out." I asked what was it like having to compete with so many brothers and sisters. Like all families, she said, we had good days and bad days, but the majority were good. "First, we loved one another very much; family came before all else. Second, my parents tried to give each and every one of us equal attention and those things we needed, but that wasn't always possible. Never having enough money, we had to share everything at least three times."

"Like hand-me-downs?" I asked. "Exactly."

Feeling I was gaining an ally, I asked her to pursue the subject of competition and having to live in the shadows of others. She said, "We had so many in our family that the shadow was more like a lunar eclipse. You have to understand and accept the fact that life isn't always going to be as fair as we would like it to be. But for every disadvantage there tends to be some kind of compensation, for every minus a plus. What do you think the pluses are of being the youngest?" I gave her my you've-got-to-be-kidding look. Sensing my skepticism, she offered some thought starters.

"Who is responsible for watching you when we're not at home?" My *brother.* "Who plays ball with you every day and includes you in his group of personal friends?" My *brother again.* "Who's the first to defend you when we want to take away privileges for misbehaving?" *Mr. Wonderful.* "And, who do we expect to set the perfect example of behavior for his younger brother?" Beaten into submission, I groaned, "I get the point." She said in her tenderest voice, "I'm not telling you these things to make you feel guilty or imply your brother is perfect; he isn't, but who is? Whenever you're feeling upset about what you think to be unfair, remember there is always another side to the story."

Once again, the sage had pulled me from the adolescent flames of self-pity and placed me safely into the hands of a developing maturity. As the years passed, so did many of my feelings of inadequacy and anonymity.

With growing maturity we learn that comparisons have no bearing on how well we perform or are perceived in life. For in the final analysis, each of us must stand alone when determining his worth, and to think otherwise only serves as a debilitating and unnecessary distraction. I do want to mention, however, that a small amount of constructive sibling rivalry is not without its rewards. I grew to be two-and-a-half inches taller than my brother. Notwithstanding that fact, his stature-and-heart will never fall short in my eyes. His lifelong devotion to education has carried him to a professorship at a highly respected private college in Pittsburgh. And finally, I've come to realize that he was, and continues to be, one of my most devoted allies.

As the years pass, I've become convinced that the insidious seeds of jealousy never really die. They may lie dormant in our minds over time but stand ready to sprout with little or no warning, and in many cases out of an absurd cause.

My Aunt Mary, my mother's older sister, tells a wonderful story about a jealous colleague who best illustrates this point. I'll refer to her as Mrs. N. V. S. My aunt was actively involved in politics for many years and was one of the leading political figures in Pennsylvania. During the Carter administration, she was a frequent visitor to the White House to consult with the President. She never boasted or even considered it as anything other than a normal part of her job. Her New York City counterpart, however, who was also a senior Democratic delegate from her district, measured her success and degree of influence against my aunt's accomplishments and contacts. And one of this woman's burning desires was to attend a luncheon with the President. She finally received an invitation to attend an *intimate* White House luncheon, along with two hundred other delegates. She couldn't wait to share the news with my Aunt Mary.

Several weeks later, at a delegate luncheon, the New Yorker spied my aunt seated with ten other prominent women. The New York woman smugly pranced up to the seated delegates and said in her unmistakable Queens accent, "Good afternoon, ladies,"—and an aside to my aunt—" . . . and you too Mary. Guess who I had lunch with the other day?" No one reacted. Undeterred, she stood at attention with her shoulders thrown firmly back, eyes aglow with pride, and declared in a tone of indubitable allegiance, "The President of the United States of America." For a brief moment, my aunt says, she expected to hear the New Yorker break out into the Star Spangled Banner.

In spite of herself, my aunt wanted to hear the details. "That's great! How was it?" she asked. "It was won-derful, if you know what I mean. The President gave such a rousing speech that he received a standing *ovulation!*" Without missing a beat, my aunt calmly responded, "Well, that is impressive!" After a momentary pause, the other women broke into uncontrollable laughter. One lady commented under her breath, "Justice is occasionally served." My aunt, however, recognized an opportunity to gain a potential convert.

She took the woman aside and explained with sensitivity why the other women were laughing. The New Yorker was totally embarrassed. My aunt told her that we all make occasional errors and that it was already forgotten. They then continued their conversation and began building a better, more positive rapport. My aunt asked her to attend some future functions that she knew the woman would enjoy and could benefit from. The invitation was eagerly accepted. It was an indication that a new relationship was in the making, and one that I might add is truly worthy of a standing ovation!

INTELLIGENCE

Mother always said, "Robert, . . .
*. . . asking good questions is
like eating a lot of fish—they
both develop great minds."*

I T WAS DINNERTIME and Mother sat expressionless as she reviewed my final grades my freshman year in college. Finally, she said, "Congratulations! They're wonderful and, just think, next year you'll be a sophomore." As I helped her clear the dinner table, I began pondering the anomaly of a woman with little education whose intelligence I would match against anyone's. Wondering about her formula for success, I said, "Mother, I have a question." "Good," she replied. "I asked her why she said *good* instead of *Yes?* "Because *Yes* doesn't tell you how important I think questions are like my father used to say, 'Asking good questions is like eating a lot of fish—they both develop great minds.' " At that moment I had a revelation that answered my question for myself. As far back as I could remember, this woman had been a human questioning machine. Her curiosity was insatiable. She read everything. She spent a lot of time deep in thought.

"Mother, but what is your reason for asking so many questions?" I asked. "Well, not having a formal education, I knew I had to assume the responsibilitiy for educating myself, and there was only one way to do that—by reading everything I could lay my hands on and learning from the experiences." I wasn't convinced. "You know when someone in school asks a lot of questions, they're labeled a brown noser or a bookworm." She laughed and said, "I can see things haven't changed from when I was in school. But you have to look beyond what children say because their opinions won't count once you're out in the world and having to make a living."

I inquired as to how she knew what questions to ask. She paused, thinking, then said, "My general rule of thumb is: Just ask those that are necessary to satisfy your needs at a given time. People don't mind answering questions as long as they feel you are interested. Also, always have a goal when you ask questions. For example, when I asked my boss about the store's inventory, I had a specific purpose in mind. Remember, don't ask more questions than you can handle. It's the same principle I teach you when you sit down to eat. Only take as much as you can finish, then if you're still hungry you can always go back for more. It's the same with learning."

Satisfied, I said, "I used to get so irritated when you'd answer my questions with another question, but now I understand why. Your questions made me think, justify my views and deal with issues, while keeping emotions in proper perspective. In addition, I usually remembered the lesson much longer. It's strange, but the older I get, the smarter you become." For once she didn't respond with a question, but maybe that was her way of telling me I had finally learned the lesson.

Her approach became an active part of every phase of my personal and business development. It was particularly useful in a city that thrives on answering questions with questions: New York, New York.

The fashion trade on the West Side of New York City is a country in itself. Watching daily activities on the street and in the buildings can't help but remind you of one of the most studied and intelligent societies known to science: an ant colony. At first glance, the ants appear to be scurring about with little purpose. When put under the microscope of scientific analysis, however, the ant colony is revealed as a finely tuned organization geared to maximum productivity. My involvement in the West Side ant colony centered around representing a large textile manufacturer. Specifically, I would interview distributors in hopes of placing my client's goods in their lines. It became especially enjoyable after I had built up rapport with the distributors and mutual respect.

A typical sales call gave one the feeling of being in an echo chamber. I would ask the question that frequently begins New York conversations, "So how's business?" The usual response was: "How should it be? Are you writing a book, or what?" I'd persist with, "Really, how is it going?" Response: "So you really want to know?" A nod. In what approached a lament, I would hear: "You should have such pain. I wouldn't wish today's market on my worst enemy, unless of course he was my major competitor."

This seemingly meaningless colloquial bantering served two important purposes. First, it was tradition, and second, it served as a positioning tool before hard negotiations got under way. One of my favorite experiences was with a dealer who never varied from his approach. For three years he would ask the same questions, and I would answer with the same questions. It was not so much a game as a means to either wearing down my position or assessing if there had been any changes in the pricing policy of the company I represented.

His initial remarks revolved around how tough business was and how much his costs had risen. I would acknowledge, but not necessarily agree with his comments. He would then ask me to show him the prices on staple goods from which he reaped consistently high margins of profit. This didn't, however, deter him from bargaining for a better deal. He would ask, "So, Robert, what are you going to do for me this year on price?" I'd smile and say, "The same thing I did for you last year, a fair price that will still meet your profit-margin objectives." He'd then say, "You know business is tough. Try and keep a kid in Harvard, a house in the Hamptons and a driver. It's not easy." My immediate reaction—wanting to laugh—was quelled by reminding myself that everything in life is relative. Instead, I answered with a question: "What do you think might happen if I gave you a lower price?" "You'd make me happy." "True, but don't you think I'd have to offer the same price to my other customers?" That didn't satisfy him. He retorted with, "Maybe so, but you represent one of the largest textile manufacturers in the business. You should be able to do better than the others. Right?" Shrug. "Maybe so, but let me ask you a question. What's the biggest reason you do so much business with us?" Eyebrow raised. "Simply the quality of your goods." I continued, "And what do you think might suffer the most if we began lowering our prices to be more price competitive?" Lips pursed. "Well . . . you have a point, but . . ." I then said, "Lower prices would be nice, but what might be the ultimate cost?" He thought for a long moment and said, "I might not be able to do the volume of business I'm presently doing if the quality began to slip." We both paused and began smiling at each other. He then said, "Well, it never hurts to ask," I looked at my watch and noticed it was lunchtime. I offered to buy.

Stating as opposed to asking can save time, but Mother's advice was always to ask. Experience had convinced her that a properly phrased question is equal or greater in value. She believed most people would prefer being asked than told, and a question can have a greater influence and staying power than most statements of fact. A good question can reduce tension, set the stage for a productive conversation and, most importantly, educate through one of the least expensive, but priceless methods: learning from the experience of others.

HUMILITY

Mother always said, "Robert, . . .
. . . there is no one more important or less
important than you. And always remember,
when you become full of yourself,
you become full of it."

I F THERE IS ONE QUALITY that cut through all
other values Mother taught, it was humility. Mother
looked beyond its obvious benefit of reducing the
amount of verbal fertilizer in the world. She perceived it
as the fulcrum for maintaining emotional and practical
balance in life. Whenever Mother sensed the slightest
nuance of the "I'm-so-important-just-ask-me" syndrome,
she would tell a story about two big . . . slimy green . . .
monsters! Mr. *LookatMe* and Mr. *ListentoMe*.

One day when I was being less than modest about a
recent accomplishment, she sat me down, practically on
her lap, and mimicking a little boy's voice, said, "Robert,
being so pleased with yourself doesn't make Mommy or
anybody happy. In fact, it annoys people so much that

they don't want to listen to you, or spend any time with you, and that hurts friendships. And worst of all, it opens the door to that big, bad green monster Mr. *LookatMe*. His job is to keep you so self-centered that you can't see left or right. His cousin, Mr. *ListentoMe*, plugs your ears to any new information or ideas from others, and lets only YOU speak and speak and (yawn) speak." To this she would add in lovingly soft tones, "Robert, sweetie. You know what you know, but that's all that you know. So my darling,"—with clenched teeth—"TRY BEING QUIET SOMETIMES AND LISTEN TO WHAT OTHER PEOPLE HAVE TO SAY!" While gently stroking the hair on her precious little boy's head, she suddenly yanked both his ears and said, "You see, sweetheart. God gave you two ears and one mouth for a reason,"—while staring impatiently into my eyes—"TRY USING THEM OCCASIONALLY!!"

The results were as follows: My ears slowly returned to their original position, and once again I humbly submitted to her point. She concluded by saying, "Now, where would you like to go tonight for your birthday dinner?" (I had just turned twenty-five!)

Mother believed in an occasional refresher. In this case it was to take place years later while the Popovich family of four surrounded a large bird that was appropriately dressed for the occasion. It was Thanksgiving.

I had just returned from completing a small but successful consulting engagement for a French company in Paris. The initial table comments covered general health and happiness questions. Everyone's cholesterol and blood pressures were at acceptable levels. This was followed by the most important quality-control check, "The Parental Happy With Their Children Level Check (PHWTCLC)."

The criterion for measuring this level is the frequency with which a child calls his parents. My brother was in the upper-fifth percentile, in other words, excellent. My PHWTCLC level fell somewhere between pestilence and famine. It was so bad that one time when I entered the house and greeted my parents (and in my own defense I must say that it couldn't have been over a month since I . . . well maybe two months, or was it three? Well, anyway, I think of them a lot!), Mother handed me a copy of a birth certificate that verified that she was indeed my birth mother. Subtlety has always been one of her major strengths.

On this occasion the dinner clock indicated that we were nearing the half-time, which meant Mother was getting bored and ready for more stimulating conversation. For openers she said, "So, how was the trip to Paris?" I knew that this ostensibly harmless question could be a potential setup, but I felt confident I could handle it. I retorted with a response that was both safe and accurate: "It went O.K." "Just O.K.?" she said. "Don't be polite. I'm really interested." Now I knew I was in trouble. I thought to myself, What is the fox up to. "Well," she said, "was your client pleased with the results?" I attempted a modest smile to mask my true feelings and said, "I'd have to say they were. In fact, it would have been difficult for them not to be pleased."

I started to recount my client's objectives, my efforts and the eventual outcome. On this particular trip, everything had gone extremely well—had fallen neatly into place. I was on, and so was the client. Recounting my triumph was truly a moment to be savored, but one I began to gnaw on. My chest began to swell and my modest pride turned into a magnificent obsession. I went on to describe every detail of my Arc de Triomphe. I was on a roll. Try and hide a smug look; it's impossible. She could sense it, as only a mother can, and said, "You're really proud of yourself, aren't you?" I said, "YES!" She continued, "You probably made all the difference in the world, huh?" By now I was gushing with pride, which bordered on wonderfulness. As the helium in my chest began to lift me off the floor, she pulled out her humility needle and said, "Well, I'm proud of you too, but we've been talking about this for over thirty minutes and I think that's long enough. Now, Robert, let me tell you a story about a big, green monster called, Mr. ListentoMe . . ." Long forgotten, but instantly remembered, I joined mother in simultaneous laughter.

When I had a moment to reflect on this lesson, an interesting thought came to mind. I had never before realized that dealing with success can be as difficult or more difficult to handle than the efforts made to achieve it. There seems to be a fine line between natural, healthy pride and overconfidence. The most difficult part of this process is not only recognizing it when it occurs, but being able to return to the other side of the line. As a result of this incident, whenever I look into a mirror, I make a special effort to focus on my ears.

PERSUASION

Mother always said, "Robert, . . .
. . . the easier you make it for me to buy,
the more likely it is that I will."

IF PEOPLE HAD TO CHOOSE just one skill to
possess, it might well be the ability to persuade others of
the value of their ideas or personal worth. In every phase
of our lives, we are constantly communicating with
others in order to achieve one of these goals. Mother
had a theory about making it easy for someone to buy an
idea or product. Her seemingly simplistic premise based
on sound psychological theories of persuasion.

Persuasion is commonly thought to be contingent on
three elements: 1. the number of things required to
make the idea happen, 2. the value it brings to those
involved, and 3. the monetary and emotional costs. My
favorite illustration of the technique of persuasion is my
mother's use of these three principles to convince my

father to go at long last on a continually postponed family vacation.

The purpose of vacations is fun, relaxation and entertainment. However, gaining agreement among all family members as to when it would be most convenient to go can be exasperating. Whenever my mother brought up the subject, my father would say, "You're right. We'll have to sit down one of these days and discuss it, but you know, the timing has to be just right." Well, as with many things in life, the right time never came. Some other priority or need always took precedence. After weeks of delays and frustration, Mother decided to follow her own advice and developed a plan.

It was an ordinary evening at the dinner table when she brought up the subject. My father used his standard line, "The timing is so important." Much to his surprise, Mother countered with, "You're right, but I have great news! The children have a long weekend coming up. It would be ideal to spend it at Niagara Falls. What do you think?" He said that would be great, but he thought she had to work. She replied that she would be able to get the time off. (*First step satisfied.*) But what about a place to stay; wasn't it too late to reserve space in a hotel? No, she said, she had checked and found a wonderful hotel on the Canadian side where it would be possible to get reservations. (*Second step completed.*) "But who'll watch the dog? He hates kennels!" Mother said our neighbor was more than willing. (*Third step in the bag. All Phase I requirements met.*)

Father began to sense that Mother had done her homework, so he started bringing out the heavy artillery. "What is there to do at Niagara that will satisfy everyone?" (*Ah! The "personal value" question. He thought he had her on this one.*) She proceeded to list everyone's preferences and guaranteed that each one would be met—even his desire to go bowling at midnight. (*Phase II completed.*) The pressure began to show. Mother was now serving for the match.

There were only two remaining issues, but they were the toughest in any match: *price and ego.* Father said, "It all sounds great, but who's going to pay for this wonderful weekend?" Mother paused for a long time. Father's eyes began to sparkle. He thought he had won with this one, but it was not to be. She said, "I knew this would be a major concern, but you know what, I was able to get a family weekend special. I reserved two rooms for the price of one, and meals are included! Isn't that great!" Ouch! He made a last-ditch effort by asking who was going to drive. Mother volunteered to share that responsibility. Sensing his impending defeat, she softened the fall with, "I want this time away for all us, not just myself and the children. You need this time away as much as we do." He nodded. (*Phase III completed. Game, set and match!*) Mother looked across the table with a small but telling smile, and said, "Boys, it's time to do your homework. I've already done mine." We broke into laughter, and Father was laughing the loudest.

I have had the opportunity to apply principles of persuasion throughout my business career, but no instance is as memorable as the case of mistaken identity, which turned into one of the most enjoyable experiences in my career.

It was Christmastime in New York, and I just left a client's office to do some shopping during lunch. It was a cold and blustery day, but as usual I wasn't wearing a coat. I find them cumbersome and uncomfortable. Better to get pneumonia than be practical. After dodging taxis and pedestrians, I reached my destination—Bloomingdales, the holiday mecca of tradition, style, prestige and warmth.

As usual, the crowds were enormous. Some find the holiday mayhem disconcerting; I find it invigorating. I weaved past bodies and shopping bags to the men's suit department. For a moment I stood motionless, savoring the spirit of the captains of industry, fashion, theater and literature who had shopped here before me. But my reverie was abruptly interrupted by an unexpected inquiry.

I was confronted by a tall, handsome, polite young

man who asked if I worked in that department. It must have been the absence of a coat. After all, it was twenty degrees outside, so his assumption seem valid. Over the years I must have been asked that same question dozens of times. I have come to feel as though I have an indelible nametag on my body that says, "I Work Here." My initial irritation for some inexplicable reason was replaced by a moment of whimsy. I replied, "Yes. How may I help you?" Maybe going through my head was some thought like, What the heck, if I can help this young man, it might turn a routine shopping junket into a more interesting and memorable one. At that moment I noticed an actual sales clerk observing this scenario. His face was a combination of confusion and curiosity.

The customer looked like a recent graduate entering the world of business for the first time, in dire need of a good suit. His attitude was the classic combination of supreme confidence along with assertiveness laced with inexperience and self-doubt.

My first question was, Why was he buying the suit? He confirmed my guess. He was a recent graduate of MIT's school of engineering and had just taken a position with Gulf Oil in Louisiana. Specifically, he would be a supervisor on an offshore drilling rig, but he would be required to make a monthly presentation to senior management on the quality and grade of the oil production. It was his first job, first suit, and, potentially, his first department store charge account. Before that step could occur, however, I needed to determine the style and price range he was looking for. He wanted a suit that would fit all occasions—business, weddings, graduations, formal affairs and funerals. All for one, and one for all.

He was a perfect forty-two long. He was in luck. Bloomies had one of the best off-the-rack custom suits you can buy—Hickey Freeman—on sale. Normally priced from $450 to $800, they were marked down for a limited time to $375 and most of those on sale were his size. I suggested he open a charge account. I then asked the sales clerk to assist him in completing the application. At that point the clerk apparently assumed I was one of the buyers and willingly assisted. (*First step satisfied.*)

Next was determining which suit he would purchase. Based upon his short- and long-term personal and business needs it was in his best interest to take two suits: navy blue and brown. This would provide greater versatility and create less wear than having just one. Also, he would always have a fresh suit available while the other was at the cleaners. With the sale price he could almost purchase two suits for the price of one. (*All of Phase II requirements met.*)

The last part was Phase III: actual and psychological costs. I assured him that he was getting a rare bargain.

He agreed. We then spent some time reviewing his budget and concluded that he could comfortably meet the monthly payments, even on his initial salary. He seemed very relaxed and comfortable with that decision. (*Phase III completed. Game, set and match!*)

At this point I turned the sale over to my loyal observer. Working on commission, he was grateful for the sale, but he wanted to know who I was. I said I was a visiting buyer only in the store for the moment and would probably never be seen again. He felt comfortable with my explanation. Why not, we were in New York City!

As I entered the elevator to exit the store, I reflected on what had just occurred. My first reaction was how much I had enjoyed the whole affair. My second thought, however, was how Mother would have evaluated this event. She would have been a bit squeamish about my assumed identity, but I'm sure the outcome would have been acceptable. She always emphasized that the intent of our behavior is the barometer for our actions. If the motives are to bring a positive outcome to all interested parties, then the action is considered acceptable. In this case, the customer got what he wanted: 1. his first charge account, 2. two suits at bargain prices, and 3. a giant step toward beginning his career on a positive high-image note. The sales clerk was equally satisfied. He received on-the-job training and a nice commission. For myself, it was an opportunity to put Mother's principles into practice once again and have a little fun in the process.

Admittedly, I did pay a price. I forgot to do my own shopping!

DIGNITY

Mother always said, "Robert, . . .
*. . . most people can survive the loss of most
things in life, but the loss of self-respect and
dignity is too great a price for anyone to pay."*

WHILE GROWING UP, I spent a great deal of
time in the shoe store where my mother worked. I
watched and analyzed her techniques for making a sale.
It was truly a work of art. To this day I marvel at how
she could wait on numerous customers at one time, and
yet make each one feel as though she were only waiting
on him. Part of this was her acute sensitivity to each
customer's unique needs. She had a special relationship
with each and every person that walked in the door.
Initial topics focused on the health of each family
member and the more important developments in their
lives. Marriages and newborns were two of the favorite
subjects. The purchasing of shoes appeared secondary.
No matter what their nationality, station in society or

personal beliefs, she treated each of them with dignity and respect.

One day Mrs. Goldberg, a lifelong friend and customer, spied the new spring line in the window. The shoes came in a variety of pastels, and it became evident that Mrs. Goldberg would probably take several pairs. It was unfortunate, however, that the new styles only came in narrow and regular widths, while her size ran more to the snowshoe category. It's interesting that when people initially have only a passing interest in buying something and then discover that it's unattainable, often it becomes an obsession. In this instance, it was to become a magnificent one.

Mother gave Mrs. Goldberg the widest width the store had in stock. Mrs. Goldberg's eyes were glittering with anticipation. I had never seen her so elated. As the right shoe neared its target, it became glaringly obvious that a mismatch was at hand. She struggled and pulled, wiggled and turned, but it wouldn't go on. She was like one of Cinderella's stepsisters frantically trying to cram her foot into the glass slipper. When she broke into a sweat, Mother, knowing her customer's history of high blood pressure, became concerned. She said, "Molly, would you like to look at some other styles?" No response. She had reached the point of no return; she was possessed. Determined, she finally had both shoes on, if "on" is defined by all of her toes being hidden and two-thirds of the heel in.

Although tired and worn, she looked like she was feeling the thrill of victory, until my mother said, "How do they feel, Molly?" The response came in a tone reminiscent of someone stuck between two Sumo wrestlers, "Great!" —gasp!—"They're just a l-i-t-t-l-e tight in the heel," Another gasp. Keeping her face expressionless, Mother said, "Good. Please stand up so I can check them." Mrs. Goldberg slowly, carefully, began to rise. She looked like a novice acrobat balancing on top of a ballpoint pen. She teetered and tottered, but finally made it. You could sense another thrill of victory, but the painful reality began to set in. Her facial expression sent the clear message that the agony of defeat was a heartbeat away, but she would not go down without a fight. After all, she had made a big investment up to that point and understandably wanted to realize a return.

Freudian theory states that each of us has an ego. Some, however, have an "eggo"— a double dose. When it came to being in fashion, Mrs. Goldberg was working on 4 G's. She wasn't just a fashion plate, she was a service for twelve. She wanted relief, but not at the expense of her 4 G's. She said, "Dorothy, you know what I look good in. What do you think?" I knew, then, that the battle was over. I anxiously waited to learn another lesson from the master of diplomacy. My mother paused for a long moment studying the shoes, and slowly said, "Well, Molly, you k-n-o-w I've *never* really liked you in pastels." Mrs. Goldberg breathed a sigh of relief and said, "You're right! Neither do I." The shoes were dismissed, her ego was left intact, and a better fit was produced. Mother's technique had truly been a work of art.

Later that evening Mother and I were discussing Mrs. Goldberg. I reminded her that she had always stressed that honesty is the best policy, and I felt as though she hadn't been totally honest. She admitted that she understood my point of view, but she added that there were other factors involved. First, it's important to recognize and be sensitive to something more precious than money can buy: self-respect and dignity. Second, the sale would have resulted in Mrs. Goldberg's dissatisfaction and eventual return of the shoes. In that case, both parties would experience a loss. Finally, when someone has their heart set on something, it's difficult to let go without some degree of satisfaction or justification.

Many years passed, and I was to experience a similar lesson in a totally different setting. It was in West Berlin and an extraordinary street juggler was practicing his craft with more than just his skill hanging in the balance.

Berlin is a haven for amateur entertainers, and during the height of the tourist season, I would enjoy watching the many different acts on every corner. On this day, I was taken by a juggler extraordinaire. Not only did he exhibit unerring dexterity, he accompanied his craft with a spontaneous monologue of one liners that had the crowd mesmerized. At the end of his performance, he received a thunderous ovation. As is customary, he passed his hat, but this day as he began working the first row of the crowd, many balked at his request. The second row, in which I was standing, would never be given a chance to contribute. Initially, he wasn't disturbed, but the pattern inexplicably continued. His eyes filled with total disbelief and justifiable resentment. He slowly lowered his hat and turned away from the audience.

Without a word, he started gathering his paraphernalia. Some members of the audience, driven more by guilt than generosity, attempted to interrupt with an offering. In German, he politely but firmly said, "No, thank you. You keep it. I don't want charity; I just wanted your respect and appreciation, but apparently I got neither." Again and again others tried, but to no avail. He was obviously deeply hurt and shaken. I waited until most of the audience had dispersed before making my attempt. I didn't know quite how to approach him, so I waited and watched for an opening.

He eventually regained his composure and began preparing for his next performance. In German, I quietly asked if this had ever happened to him before. He appeared rather surprised, but shook his head. I then asked, "It's difficult at times to understand why people act as they do. Yes?" Again he nodded, but this time affirmatively. At that point, for what it was worth, I felt compelled to offer my critique. I said, "Well, for me I thought you were not only skilled, but extraordinarily gifted. The monologue and impromptu comments were exceptional." He smiled modestly, and thanked me.

I then asked why he had so adamantly refused the offers that the audience subsequently made. He repeated that it was because they were giving out of guilt and pity, and not out of true appreciation for his work. They had insulted his honor, and no amount of money could be an adequate compensation. I told him that I understood and respected his actions. As I was about to leave, I offered him a contribution which he initially refused. I assured him it was solely an acknowledgment for his efforts, and for no other reason. He finally accepted, and simply said thank you.

As I turned to walk away, a new crowd was already forming. Even though no one could predict how this audience would react, I was certain that the juggler would always respond with quiet dignity.

REALITY

Mother always said, "Robert, . . .
. . . deal with what is and not
what you think should be."

IN MY YOUTH I would always ask the same question when things didn't go my way, "But why, Mom? Why does it have to be that way?" And if she said it once, she said it a million times, "Because that's just the way it is! I've explained the reasons to you, but you're not willing to accept them. Now, please don't ask me again!" She was right as usual, but I never wanted to admit it. My supposition was that if I kept asking over and over again, the situation might change, and I'd get what I wanted. But it never quite worked out that way. My frustrations were a function of not *wanting to accept the reality of a particular situation*. She would say, "Robert, if you deal with what *is* and not what you think *should* be, you will not only eliminate the problem much more quickly, but you'll also be less frustrated, much happier and more productive."

This particular counsel had far-reaching implications for me during my youth. Some of the more devastating were school-related. For example, being advised that a term paper in history was due two weeks earlier than originally scheduled, my first reaction was, "This isn't fair! How could he do this to me!" He had, and that's the only thing that mattered at that point. Although I knew the date wouldn't change, it took me at least two days to get over my frustration before I started to work toward meeting the shorter deadline. Not only did I waste two days, but I was so focused on negative thoughts that once I finally accepted the fact, it took another two days to gain a positive attitude and the momentum to complete the project. Mother observed my reactions but said nothing. She recognized that my state of mind was at its least-receptive state. She knew I had to go through the natural course of anger and self-pity before reaching eventual acceptance.

After I completed the paper just one day before the due date, she asked to have a little chat. Mother's little chats usually meant counseling time—but I really didn't mind because they were generally short and to the point, and meaningful. She started off by asking how I felt about completing the paper on time. I said I was just glad it was over. She agreed. She then asked what I had learned from this experience. "Never to trust teachers." I replied. She smiled and asked if I really meant that. I said no, but I just felt it was so unfair. She reminded me that many things in life are unfair, but if they can't be changed then the only option is to deal with them, whether we like it or not. And the quicker we attack a problem, the quicker it goes away. I admitted, "I guess you're right." But then she asked what else I might have learned. I said maybe not to waste time pouting over something that's not going to change by trying to wish it away. "As you always say, Mother, deal with what is and not what you think should be. Right?" She smiled, "There's still hope for you." Lesson duly noted—one that would eventually make its way to Stuttgart, West Germany, where a down market provided an opportunity for an engineering firm to stop pouting and start taking advantage of reality.

I was asked to speak at a workshop conference for the management of an American engineering company that was experiencing an unexpected downturn. Business had suddenly dropped off by 25 percent and, needless to say, management was very concerned. I asked what they were doing to deal with the situation. Their response wasn't totally unexpected. All personnel had been advised to cut back immediately on expenditures. That meant no travel, plus counting staples and rubberbands.

I then asked what formal announcements had been made advising the employees of the severity of the situation. They said none because they didn't want to alarm anyone unnecessarily. They knew that this would all pass in time, and things would eventually return to normal. I questioned this strategy because it is generally known that the frontline personnel are usually the first to know what the state of business is, and using subterfuge to avoid panic would in fact, create a deeper problem than the downturn itself was doing. They asked what that worse problem might be. I said loss of respect for management. By not attacking the situation honestly, i.e., dealing with what is and not what they wanted things to be, in their noble attempt to avoid creating anxiety, they were actually creating more. If they would deal with events in an honest, open and direct manner, they could actually take advantage of the situation. They asked how. I said I would need a little time to develop my ideas, so we took a break. I thought to myself, "Robert, this better be good." In asking them to look at reality, I found myself having to do the same. One of the company officers walked up to me as I was preparing my notes and said with a wry smile, "You've piqued our curiosity; now we expect you to satisfy it."

We reconvened and you could sense the intensity of expectation. I began with, "Mother always said, 'Robert, deal with what *is*, not what you think *should* be.' " I continued by saying that every business will have its difficult times, and how you handle those downturns will set the tone when business begins to improve. In fact, it sometimes can serve as a catalyst for making the turnaround occur sooner than expected. And it can give a kick to the forward momentum as well. It's the attitude you bring to the situation, I said, that will determine the actions that you take in a tough market.

I then asked a question, "What if you heard the following announcement when times were tough? How would you react? 'Ladies and gentlemen, we are experiencing a *temporary* drop in business. None of us knows how long this situation will persist, but that's not what's important at this point. *Our objective is to see how we can take advantage of the situation.* This gives us an excellent opportunity to do some things that we normally don't have time to do when business is good. For example, we can: 1. conduct an in-depth analysis of how well we are serving our existing customer base 2. identify and develop strategies for serving them better 3. define new business development strategies and 4. review and assess our existing marketing plan and make any necessary adjustments. In addition, we can review and update, where needed, internal operational procedures, policies and systems. And finally, we can review and improve working relationships between departments.' "

I went on to explain that the specific content wasn't the point of the illustration. It was the intent and potential effect this type of announcement would have on employees. It is during times like these when a company has an opportunity to show its true character and capability for leadership. In addition, the announcement serves as a model of behavior for every individual and department when they address their own daily challenges. For in the final analysis, Mother would say, it's how you react under pressure that people will long remember. By coming through under pressure, management can develop better long-term motivation and loyalty from its employees.

We surveyed the room and a consensus was reached, *an acceptance and willingness to implement this strategy.* It wasn't a vote of confidence for Mother or myself, but for the individuals in the room who recognized that dealing with reality in the most direct and positive manner is a more effective and efficient way of conducting business, no matter what the circumstances.

COMMUNICATION

Mother always said, "Robert, . . .
*. . . if you don't till the soil before you plant
the seeds, they just wash away and
you've wasted your time."*

M other's rural heritage predisposed her to use farming-related sayings to illustrate her lessons. One of her favorites was, "If you don't till the soil before you plant the seeds, they just wash away and you've wasted your time." She felt the same principle applied when communicating with people. If you properly till the mental soil of your listener by planting your thoughts or ideas, the quality of the exchange will be dramatically improved. She also said it gave people fewer places to hide. This was especially true every time the topic was school and my grades.

At the end of each grading period, she would advise me that it was time again for one of her favorite discussions: "Let's Review the Grades." (*Not one of my*

favorite subjects, but at least I knew to expect it.) Before
she would begin, however, she would make sure I had a
chance to talk about how I thought I had done so that I
wouldn't be too apprehensive. *(Hmmm! Rather
impressive, considering she's my mom and the boss.)* She'd
continue with, "We need to see where you're doing well
and where you're not doing so well." *(Sounds fair to me.
Good points and bad points.)* I said, "Well, I think I did
pretty well: 3 A's; 3 B's; and 3 C's." She said on average
that wasn't bad, but what were the subjects? *(Details.
Why did she always have to bring up details?)* She asked to
see the report card. *(Why couldn't she just take my word
that they were evenly distributed among all my subjects?)*
"Hmmm!" she said as her eyes lit on the first grade. "An
'A' in English." Then the next: "An 'A' in Citizenship."
(Behavior is in order.) But then she said, "I certainly
wouldn't expect anything less in that category." *(So no
points there.)* "An 'A' in Gym." Her eyes told me her
estimation and knowledge of physical education was
limited to having to buy my new sneakers.

At this point she realized I had run out of A's and all
other subjects had to fit 3 B's and 3 C's. "A 'B' in
Geography" *(I know an ocean when I see one).* She sort
of smiled at that one. "A 'B' in Art." (Ahh! Four field
trips a year!) "A 'B' in Music." *(Chorus was always one of
my strengths.)* Her expression was mixed, somewhere
between "That isn't bad" to her spectacular "I've-just-

run-out of "A's and B's" look. "A 'C' in Math." (*I had a premonition that calculators would come along some day.*) She wasn't smiling. "A 'C' in Science. And a 'C' in Handwriting."

With the preliminaries out of the way, the duel began. She asked if I was pleased. I countered with, "I'm pleased if you're pleased. Are you?" She parried with, "What do you think?" Nervously I defended with, "I don't know." She went on the offensive with, "Why don't you?" I said, "Because!"

Well, I survived the duel, with an admonition that the distribution of grades had to be realigned. She offered some helpful hints and concluded with a summary of what she wanted me to do and checked my understanding by making me repeat her instructions in my own words. After numerous clarifications, the talk had ended. (*It's always tough when mothers use logic and polite, firm tones when they talk to you. It doesn't leave many bushes to hide behind.*)

Even though these situations weren't always pleasant, I considered them less threatening and more productive than I would have if she had handled them differently. I went through so many of these sessions that the process couldn't help become a permanent fixture in my mind and eventually served me well in my business career. One particular case was during an annual review of my performance early in my career.

Annual reviews have never been a favorite with those doing the evaluating or with those being evaluated. Even with some of today's sophisticated evaluation systems, there is still that critical factor of human emotion which is never wholly predictable or easy to deal with. This is often the reason evaluators try to get through the process in as little time as possible and with as little conflict as necessary.

My boss was unfortunately not an exception to the rule. He had an uncanny ability to schedule reviews for the last ten minutes of the day, just prior to him leaving for the airport for a trip to some destination that required multiple visas and shots, not to mention there being one flight a month, with a triple cancellation fee. One of these reviews occurred after I had just had one of my best years. I was, for once, looking forward to my evaluation so eagerly that I had forgotten about his typical strategy.

He called me on a Friday and said he wanted to see me at exactly five p.m. sharp. I found out from his secretary that he was leaving that evening for an unknown destination in Asia on a 6:30p.m. flight. Allowing a half hour to get to the airport, I knew my time was so limited that I would have to take my best shot early in the discussion. I entered his office with what I thought was a fail-safe approach. Well, the best-laid plan turned into folly. Before I had even sat down, he said, "Look, Robert, I don't have much time. I just want you to know that I think you're a nice, hardworking guy, and that you did a darn good job for us this year." At the same time he handed me a frugal-looking piece of paper that had a percentage raise written on it that was small enough to nearly qualify me for food stamps. Then he mentioned the time of his flight, not once but at least three times. Even though I had anticipated and prepared for this strategy, it was still disconcerting. Nevertheless, I held my ground.

All the while thinking of my mother (at least she would have gone through my report card, subject-by-subject, grade-by-grade), I tried to think of what could be used to soften his mental terra firma. I was so preoccupied that he must have asked at least three times, "Robert, what is it? Are you all right?" I apologized and said that I just needed a moment to gather my thoughts. And I did. I picked out one of Mother's favorite plows and began tilling his soil.

I tried very hard to divorce myself from the situation by saying, "Mr. Jones, I recognize your time constraints, but I was wondering if I could take just fifteen minutes of your time to share my thoughts on my evaluation from both of our perspectives. I thought we might take a quick look at specific requirements and then assess what I did well, and maybe not so well. In that way I'll be better able to understand your expectations and perceptions of my work. From there, I hope you might share with me some of your experience on how I might be able to improve, which will better equip me to keep meeting your and the company's goals." I assured him that he'd have plenty of time to get to the airport. He sat back and said, "Ahh . . . sure, go ahead, but you understand it's got to be quick." I said no problem.

I began listing the specific goals in my job description, along with the numbers my department had achieved. One by one, step-by-step, we covered what was expected and the scheduled percentage increases for achieving each goal. We also covered many areas in which I needed to improve. By focusing on specific issues, we avoided personal conflicts. Quite interestingly, his perceptions were very insightful. We shared the responsibility and dealt with the issues and not our personalities. It worked like a charm.

Mother always stressed that the beginning of a conversation is usually the most important part of any discussion. She said it was important to be as objective as possible, and that was achieved by taking into consideration the needs of all interested parties. As for me, my raise went from a fraction to a whole number. As for my boss, he appeared to be pleased with the manner in which we had handled the situation. One thing I'm definitely sure of, he made his plane. I know because I drove him to the airport.

OPINIONS

Mother always said, "Robert, . . .
. . . there are three sides to every story—
two opinions and the truth."

Whenever i'd offer my opinion or
judgment about someone or something of relative
importance, Mother would always ask why I felt as I did
or what facts I based my opinion on. I'd usually become
a little defensive and say, "Can't I have a personal
opinion?" She'd respond, "Of course you can, dear, but I
was just curious as to how you arrived at that
conclusion." This was especially true when she sensed a
less-than-objective attitude on my part. Her approach
was effective because it was always delivered in a
constructive manner. As the years passed, I found myself
becoming more responsible for what I'd say and why I'd
say it. One day I had the opportunity to observe her
practice what she preached when she was confronted by
a customer who felt the Big Apple was full of worms.

It was a typical Saturday in Aliquippa, Pennsylvania, when a well-dressed professional-looking gentleman entered the shoe store. Mother greeted him and asked if she could be of assistance. He replied that he was attending a local fund-raiser that evening and needed a pair of dress shoes. Mother showed him several pairs she felt would meet his needs. Since he was not a regular customer, she asked if he was from out of town. "I'm originally from New England, but presently working and living in New York City." As the conversation progressed, he asked if she had ever been to New York. When she indicated that she had, he asked, "How did you find it?" She replied, "Big, exciting and full of energy." Suddenly, a scowl filled his face. "What! You must be kidding me. It's the worst city in the world!" My initial reaction was, Uh, forget this sale, but then I thought, Better not count Mother out just yet. My second reaction proved to be correct.

She showed no visible sign of defensiveness. She paused a moment and then gave him a small but disarming smile. He looked confused and then curious. She said in a nonjudgmental tone, "I'd be very interested in knowing why you feel as you do." His face beginning to look more calm, he replied, "For one thing it's very expensive. It can also be a very dangerous city. The crowds are enormous, and the traffic and noise can drive you crazy." He waited for her reaction. He didn't have to wait long. "You're right. Those can be difficult and frustrating things to deal with." Her comments were more of an acknowledgement than an agreement.

The unexpected response left him guarded. He checked for understanding by asking, "Are you saying you agree with me?" She responded, "Yes and no." Now he was totally confused. "I guess," she said, "it comes down to one's own point of view. I mean, everything you say is true to a degree, but I would think that most major cities have those types of problems." He nodded slowly. She went on, "That being the case, my attitude has always been there are positives and negatives in everything. I personally try and make the best of every situation. For example, what if anything do you find interesting, unique and enjoyable in the city?" He bit his lip, "Well, the theaters and entertainment are hard to beat." "Anything else?" she asked. "The restaurants are some of the best in the world, and the shopping is unlimited." The discussion continued for a while longer. Finally, he admitted, "I guess this confirms the old adage, 'There are two sides to every story.' " Mother smiled and said, "Oh, I was always taught there are three." He looked surprised. "Three?" My mother nodded. "Of course. Two opinions and the truth." He looked puzzled, but as the words registered, he began laughing. "You know what? You're right! I never thought of it that way." Mother made two sales that day, a pair of shoes and a pair of opinions that began moving closer to the truth.

Opinions and judgments come in many degrees of intensity and appear in a variety of situations. One of the most pleasant experiences I had ever had occurred when maturity and credibility ran head-on into youth and inexperience. The battle lines were drawn, but the final outcome resulted in both parties sharing the spoils with an unlikely heroine.

I was attending a conference in Stuttgart, West Germany, held by the US Army Corps of Engineers for local private contractors. It was designed to improve relations between the various parties and productivity. Over the years I had done a substantial amount of consulting for the Corps and would frequently attend workshops to improve my knowledge and local contacts. The speakers were well-known and respected by the audience, except for one. She was a young female engineer who specialized in the writing of contracts and their interpretation. She had an excellent reputation within the Corps but hadn't as yet proven herself with private contractors. Little did she know that she would encounter an opinion that would not only test her technical knowledge, but also her skills in international diplomacy.

She had just made her introductory comments when a

rather disgruntled and seasoned-looking gentleman raised his hand and stated, "Young lady, with no personal disrespect to you, I believe this topic requires someone who has a greater degree of experience. May I suggest a more senior member of your organization handle this portion of the presentation." Neither I nor anyone else in the audience expected such a comment, and it certainly surprised her.

Temporarily frozen by the remark, she quickly regained her composure and asked, "Sir, if I understand correctly, it's your opinion that my qualifications and experience are inadequate. Is that right?" He appeared a bit startled, but nodded affirmatively. She countered with a totally unexpected response, "Given my limited direct work experience with contractors, I understand why you have drawn that conclusion. However, I've prepared what I think will be an interesting, informative and practical presentation. My overall objective is to review proposed changes in contract policies and procedures to improve productivity and avoid costly misinterpretations for both parties. I encourage you and the other members of the conference to offer your experienced opinions to determine the value of what I suggest."

The presentation continued for approximately an hour. It was a lively discussion of existing policies and proposed changes. Each side received a fair opportunity to state their opinion. A consensus was reached on some recommendations, others were only partially acceptable, and others totally discarded. Sensing most of the presentation's objectives had been met, she announced a short coffee break.

We then returned to complete the session. At its conclusion, many of the participants made it a point to commend her on her efforts. I noticed her original antagonist waited until most of the audience had left. He walked up to her and said, "Young lady, I misjudged you. I assumed your age and experience were insufficient, but I was wrong." She acknowledged his comment by saying, "Your concern over my inexperience was basically valid. I'm just pleased I was able to bring sufficient added value to the discussion." He smiled and departed.

As she began gathering her materials, I approached her to introduce myself and offer my congratulations. She said casually, "Well, as Mother always said, there are three sides to every story, two opinions and the truth." Shocked, I said, "Excuse me, but where did you hear that?" She smiled and said, "You don't remember me, but I attended one of your workshops several years ago when you told the story of the New Yorker and your mother." "Well, that's certainly one on me," I said and we both began laughing.

MOTHER ON OPINIONS

As Mother would often remark, although opinions are generally considered personal in nature, they can serve to increase our basic credibility and degree of influence on others if based upon sound logic and facts. But of course that's just her opinion.

HUMILIATION

Mother always said, "Robert, . . .
*. . . humiliation is the worst form of
embarrassment a person can experience."*

MOTHER'S TEACHINGS COVERED many
behaviors that she found almost unforgivable, but none
as heartbreaking as one human being humiliating
another. It infringed on every personal and religious
belief she had. She considered it one of the most
degrading forms of embarrassment anyone could
experience or witness. She would say, "Once you've
been humiliated, you may be able to forgive, but it's
unlikely you'll ever forget." I once asked her why it was
so terrible. She said, "Because it takes away a part of
your soul and that isn't easily repaired." At the age of
eleven, I understood in a general way, but I hadn't as yet
experienced it. I felt that I would be able to recognize a
humiliating experience, but what I didn't know was how
I'd feel. It wasn't long after this discussion I found out.

Mother would often say children can be more cruel out of ignorance than adults by intent. That was difficult to understand until I witnessed it. I had always been taught that the true worth of a person isn't based on how much money he has, but what he is like as a person. To think or behave otherwise, I was taught, is contrary to what is truly of value in life. Unfortunately, not everyone feels that way.

Each day when I boarded the bus to go to school, I found most of the children occupying the same seats they sat in every day. I could also count on everyone sitting with a friend or acquaintance, except for one girl who was always alone. She sat directly behind the driver and rarely had a companion. I didn't notice for the longest time, until one day I asked one of my friends whether the girl was just shy. He said rather incredulously, "You don't know? She's the girl from down the road who wears the same dress every day. Everyone says her family doesn't even have a bathroom in their house! No one would be caught dead talking to her!"

As the year progressed, she was constantly harassed by the other children. They made fun of her unusually deep voice and the dress that she wore almost daily. Then one day the harassment got totally out of hand. A group of children formed a circle around her on the playground and began taunting her. "We don't like poor girls!" they

shouted. "Why don't you go live somewhere else?" She
stood motionless for the longest time until she finally
broke down and fell to the ground crying. One of the
teachers intervened and scattered the children. She
helped the girl to her feet and took her into the office.
At that point I knew what Mother had meant. As I had
watched the girl being taunted, I felt intense pain and
embarrassment. I couldn't imagine anyone being treated
so cruelly and still being able to return to school the
next day. But she did.

As I grew older, the circumstances were to change,
but not my feelings. I would once again witness a
person being humiliated, this time in a unique city—
West Berlin—one of the most unlikely backdrops for
such an incident because of the city's desire to erase its
historical image of violence.

When living in Berlin, I looked forward to the
coming of summer. It is the season of outdoor cafes,
seemingly endless hours of sunlight, stimulating
conversation and an indescribable serenity that fills the
heart and mind. The streets become a sea of humanity
representing every corner of the earth, and all speaking
different languages, but all one and the same in their
humanness. Prior to the dismantling of the Wall, the
city—a political island isolated only by its geography—
created a kind of bond proudly acknowledged by those
who lived there. And now that the Wall has been torn

down, the city will once again like a chameleon adapt and take on new colors and shapes, but its heart and soul will always remain—uniquely Berlin.

In spring, large crowds would form on every corner to watch jugglers, mimes and musicians practice their skills. Many of these performers are university students using their talents as a means to supplementing their income. On this particular day, I was seated at a sidewalk cafe at the famous intersection of Kurfurstendamm and Joachimsthalerstrasse. The Cafe Kranzler was packed with a supportive audience enjoying the antics of one of Berlin's finest mimes. As part of his act, the mime would intentionally walk toward an approaching passerby and when the victim passed, the mime would turn and walk directly behind them. What made it hilarious was his uncanny ability to imitate with precision their gait and mannerisms. It was superb.

Time and time again, a new individual became an unknowing victim, until the pattern was shamefully broken. A rather tall, slender man, approximately thirty years of age, was the prey. All preceded normally until the man unexpectedly turned and spat directly into the mime's face. This was followed by the man swinging wildly and striking the mime. All the while he was screaming obscenities. I along with several hundred other spectators could not believe what we were witnessing. Stunned, the mime stood frozen. A veil of silence fell, and the happiness of the day seemed hopelessly lost. The mime apologized to the attacker and slowly turned away. The stunned crowd began verbally admonishing the man's behavior and was very close to detaining him for the authorities. Sensing the crowd's fury, he rushed off. The crowd fell silent again. It was undoubtedly one of the more humiliating experiences any individual could suffer. Neither the mime nor audience uttered a word. His reaction would determine ours.

At that point, the mime raised his hands as if to gesture to the audience that he needed a couple of minutes to regroup. He walked back to his staging area, pretended to wipe off the old face, and put on a new one. Once he completed his preparation, he stood motionless looking down at the ground. That moment turned into an eternity. He could have packed up and left, and no one would have faulted him, but he didn't. He gave the crowd a big smile and continued on as though nothing had happened. The spontaneous roar from the onlookers was deafening. When he completed his performance, he made the traditional rounds with his hat for contributions. He was generously rewarded for both his unique talent and for the courage he'd exhibited. Admiration and respect filled the eyes of everyone he passed. Words of encouragement and appreciation came from all sides.

It was more than just an outstanding demonstration of courage and professionalism. The incident created an unexpected bonding between the mime and his audience. What would normally have been only a surface relationship developed into a special and personal one. And most importantly, it suggested hope for the preservation of basic human decency.

RESPECT

Father always said, "Robert . . .
*. . . respect takes a lifetime to build and
only a second to lose. It doesn't seem
quite fair, but that's the way it is."*

I T WAS A TYPICAL EARLY SUNDAY MORNING.
The night before, I had been allowed to stay up late to
watch a wonderful old movie, and now I hoped my
father might let me sleep in just a little before getting
ready for church. But that was as improbable as Mother
permitting me to be late for school. I was an altar boy
and attendance was not only mandatory but necessary.

As I turned over to enjoy the last moments of
uninterrupted slumber, I heard the familiar sound of my
bedroom door opening and I knew my father's voice
would not be far behind. Like so many times over the
years, we started the morning with a game. He would
say, *"Kimasho (let's go). . . rise and shine."* I'd respond a
Japanese phrase I had begged him to teach me, *"Mo sugu*

desu!" (Soon!) He'd reply with, *"Ima!" (Now!)* I'd start laughing and counter with another jewel, *"Ato de (later) . . . Dozo!" (please!)*. And so the game would continue until I respected his wishes and readied myself for church. At that particular moment, for some unknown reason, my thoughts were driven to think about the man who was standing before me.

Theodore Popovich, son of Eastern European immigrants and truly a man for all seasons. Father, friend, counselor, soldier, linguist and chess player extraordinaire—and more importantly, a man of impeccable humanitarian credentials and inherent humility.

Father, the silent force who shaped my basic understanding of the value he most guarded and cherished: *Respect for self and others.*

Over breakfast, Father announced the day's agenda: Church, dinner and a visit to the New Brighton home of father's Aunt Tina. Anticipating my usual protest, he said, "You know that it's very important to pay your respects to your relatives." I agreed pleasantly. He didn't know how to take this unexpected response. After all, this visit consisted of spending a hot summer afternoon in an old Victorian house. The most dreaded part was having to sit patiently on a horsehair sofa that itched miserably. The only saving grace was that my aunt was pleasant, kind and so appreciative for the time we spent with her. In addition, she always had candy and soft drinks, which were not on my parents' list of household essentials. They were into health, not fun.

This time the visit to my aunt's house went so well, that Father brought it up on the way home. He started by saying to my mother that he found Aunt Tina in good spirits and perfect health. Mother agreed. Then without warning, he seemed to be jolted by the sudden realization that I had also seemed to enjoy the afternoon. A puzzled expression on his face, he said, "Robert, you didn't seem to mind today's visit." I admitted that it hadn't been too awful. He asked what had made that day different from other days. I replied, "I don't know. Maybe I'm learning it's important to spend time with family." He smiled and said, "Whether you mean that or not, I thank you for the thought." I was beginning to internalize his feelings about respect.

All during the years I was growing up, he would often remark that respect took a lifetime to build, but only a second to lose. No matter how unfair that may seem, we logically should take great care to protect others' respect for us at all times. I once asked during my college years, "How can anyone feel comfortable with that constant threat in mind?" He laughed and said, "Actually, it really isn't as terrible as it might seem. If you just think before you speak or act, which usually means taking into account the potential consequences of your actions, you'll rarely have a problem." I found his explanation realistic and satisfying.

After entering the corporate world and subsequently becoming a consultant, I struggled with Father's concept of respect and the role I perceived for it in business. It appeared as though an individual's title, function and performance record seemed to define the respect others felt for him or her. In social settings, it didn't seem much better. Cocktail conversations usually began with "What school did you attend?" "Where do you live?" and, usually disguised in some form, "How much money do you make?" and "What connections do you have?" The respect a person commanded appeared to be reduced to the size of his or her portfolio. This was disconcerting to say the least. It shook my faith and challenged Father's teachings. I was fortunate to discover, however, that it was more a case of temporary displacement of Father's teachings than a permanent conversion.

Father's tenets did hold true, but it took an unfortunate incident to renew my faith. While attending a retreat for a professional firm, one of the senior partners, who was held in high esteem within and outside the firm, put on a display of impropriety that rivaled any I had ever witnessed.

Our table was made up of the senior partner and one other partner, plus two associates, two administrative assistants and two important clients. The unwitting star of the evening began drinking to excess. This was followed by a barrage of prejudiced comments that touched every level of society. As if that weren't enough, he began telling jokes that could only be defined as base and a total misunderstanding of the intent of humor. His behavior became so obnoxious that people at other tables not only noticed, but were visibly annoyed. He finally excused himself and left. Being a guest, I made no comment. It was obvious, however, that the group at our table felt a sense of relief and acute embarrassment.

At that moment, one of the administrative assistants offered apologies on behalf of the firm. The second assistant echoed her remarks and said, "His behavior is not representative of his true nature." One of the clients smiled politely. Subsequent discussion centered around general topics until the other client unexpectedly began discussing the importance of propriety in society. His comments centered around consideration and respect for others. As he continued, others joined in.

The discussion lasted approximately an hour, and the conclusions were quite remarkable. They ranged from a need to reevaluate the values that are truly important in life and business to the responsibility each of us has, no matter what level or position we attain, to maintain self-respect and respect for others.

This conversation might not have taken place

without the performance of the senior partner, but in any event, his behavior served as a vivid demonstration of the results of discarding respect. I never heard whether he suffered any negative feedback within the firm, but based upon Father's teachings, I can't imagine any punishment worse than that of lowering his own self-esteem. What I can assume, however, is that the people seated at our table and the others who witnessed his behavior may forgive, but won't soon forget. It is virtually assured that the level of respect he had prior to the luncheon is gone forever. As Father said, It only takes a second to lose and a lifetime to build. Most important, I now knew that the basic ingredients of Father's definition of respect were not in danger of giving way to the changing times.

EXTRA EFFORT

Mother always said, "Robert, . . .
. . . if you give more than is asked for,
you will always receive more in return."

My PARENTS' WORK ETHIC was a result of their heritage. It went beyond the standard cliché of "a fair day's pay for a fair day's work." Mother was taught that if you give more than what is expected, you will never want, nor will your employer, for reward or recognition. Although I understood in a general sort of way, I needed to know more about "more." What did it mean?

One day I asked. She appeared pleased by the question. A stroke is a stroke, and moms do like being stroked! She explained that it means more than just producing more. "More" means keeping a positive attitude and taking initiative. I gave her my I-think-I-understand-what-you're-saying look, but revealed that I didn't have a clue by saying, "Hmmm! I t-h-i-n-k I see what you mean, more or less." Sensing my confusion, she said, "Look, just remember, whatever task you are given, always try to do more than what is expected, and never ask for or expect instant rewards for your efforts. Sometimes they come quickly, and other times they may take much longer, but remember, the rewards will eventually come."

As a youngster, one of my daily tasks was to empty the garbage. And each day, I did just that. No more, no less. One day, I noticed a strong and undesirable odor coming from the waste can. At that point, for some reason, it became clear to me that something *more* needed to be done; it needed to be washed.

After emptying the garbage, I took the initiative— not only washing out the can, but also spraying it with disinfectant. Mother observed my effort and pulled out the mixer and pans. When I was finished, she said, "I just want to thank you for that extra effort in doing more than what was asked. I'm making your favorite apple pie, and it should be done in an hour." Although I appreciated the praise and reward, I felt an equally strong feeling of self-satisfaction and accomplishment. Extra effort means going that extra mile, but little did I know that one day it would require me to go an additional 4,000 to prove I had not forgotten the lesson.

I had just arrived in New York from an exhausting six-week trip through four Eastern-Block countries. It was not only physically tiring, but emotionally as well. The passport and visa requirements alone can tax the most seasoned traveler. This particular trip was even worse. My only thought was to return home for a much-needed rest, or so I thought. As I waited for my luggage in the baggage claim area, I heard an announcement on the intercom. "Your attention, please. Passenger Mr. Robert Popovich, please contact the TWA message desk immediately." Jetlagged, the page did not register initially, but when it did my first thought came in the form of a question, "How could anyone know on which flight I would be arriving?" I couldn't imagine who it might be.

It was my secretary. She said one of my clients had called in a barely controlled state of panic. She didn't know the specifics, but she had a number for me to call. He needed to speak with me immediately. After several busy signals, I finally reached him. The first thing out of his mouth was, "Robert! Am I glad I got a hold of you. We need to ask a very special favor." I thought, as long as it doesn't have to happen for at least forty-eight hours. But it did. He wanted me to fly that evening to Pittsburgh and then immediately on to Phoenix, Arizona. I couldn't believe what I was hearing. What could be so important? He explained. His company was entertaining a senior delegation of German officials the next day. He wanted me to provide translation and protocol support. He went on to say he would understand if I refused. After all, I had just been on the road for six weeks, and he knew how tired I must be, but he wouldn't be asking if it weren't critical. I agreed.

Upon arriving in Pittsburgh, I was briefed on the situation. He assured me the flight to Phoenix would be enjoyable. He had booked us on a nonstop first-class flight. We would be able to relax and discuss the details over dinner. All things considered, it shouldn't be too bad. I was wrong. It turned out to be a disaster.

As we checked in at the ticket counter, we were advised the flight to Phoenix was canceled, and we could only be rebooked on another flight leaving two hours later. Further, the only available seats were in coach and no meal would be served. As if that weren't enough, we were informed the flight would be going to Tucson, and we would have to drive to Phoenix. My client was dismayed.

Our flight arrived in Tucson at midnight. We rented a car and drove across the desert, pulling into our hotel at four o'clock in the morning. This gave us only one hour of rest before we had to dress and head for the office. Once we arrived there, I prepared a brief agenda and protocol requirements. This was done between six and seven a.m. I advised senior management that it would be polite if we would be outside when the German delegation arrived. The cool morning air served as a much-needed elixir.

The agenda was straightforward: an initial tour of the facility followed by preliminary discussions, break for lunch and then more-detailed meetings. As the sessions proceeded, it became apparent that some members of the delegation had a stronger command of the English language than others did. My role was to provide intermediary support as needed. All in all, the sessions went quite well, and both parties were more than satisfied with the outcome. At the end of the day we exchanged farewells and business cards. It was now time to return to Washington, D.C., for a much-needed rest.

My client insisted on taking me to the airport. As we were about to leave the office, he expressed his personal thanks and appreciation. He also mentioned that fees had never been discussed. I said that wasn't of major importance at the time. He smiled and handed me a sealed envelope and said, "I hope you find the compensation acceptable. Please open it and tell me if you do." I refused. I said I'm sure it would be more than fair.

As he dropped me off in front of the terminal, he again expressed his gratitude for my offering to go above and beyond the call of ordinary business expectations. I acknowledged the fact that the effort had been quite demanding, but also stated it was a small price to pay for the opportunity he had given me. Specifically, I would be an integral part of future agreements that would tie the two countries closer together. Further, it provided me with future contacts in Germany. And finally, his strong desire to have me involved was the highest form of professional respect, and that in itself was adequate compensation.

I boarded the flight and took my seat as we waited to take off. Pondering the recent events, I reached inside my left front suit pocket and pulled out the payment envelope. As I looked at the amount, I realized that just as I had given more than what was expected, they had written a check that was more than generous. So it goes.

VALUE

Mother always said, "Robert, . . .
. . . value is something everyone looks for in everything they buy or experience in their lives."

I T WAS GOING TO BE ONE of the most difficult days in my life. I had to make a choice between buying a new Boy Scout uniform or replacing my old, worn-out bicycle. My mind was spinning like a revolving door. A little voice on my left shoulder kept saying, "Take the bike. It's so much fun, and anyway, you really need it for your paper route." On the other shoulder was the voice of my entire scout troop exhorting, "It's almost jamboree time, and every scout in the entire United States will be there. Think how great it will be to have all those merit badges sewn on a bright new uniform." It was dinnertime and I sat motionless before my plate. Whenever I lost interest in food, Mother automatically knew I was facing a dilemma of overwhelming proportions.

Sensing my pain, she said, "Is something wrong?" No response. "You're looking awfully sad." Aside from an almost undetectable shrug of the shoulders, I remained inaccessible. "If you're so troubled, can't you tell me why?" Finally in a tiny voice I said, "It wouldn't do any good anyway." Whenever I made that statement, it was only a matter of time before I'd share my life-ending predicament. Like clockwork, I spilled my guts, and as always, Mother made me feel as though she was equally distressed.

After listening to my tale of woe, she said, "Well, I can certainly understand why you're so troubled. Choices can be very difficult." This was followed by, "How do you think you're going to solve this problem?" I said, "I don't know. I thought you could make up my mind." She could, but she wouldn't. She pointed out that the freedom of personal choice is very precious, and shouldn't be easily relinquished, even in the most difficult of times. I thought that was a cop-out, but Mother didn't have to try and convince me of her position; it was a parent's inalienable right.

She then said, "Let me ask you this, 'Which do you think is more important, the bicycle or the uniform?' " I really couldn't say. Sensing my frustration, Mother suggested I list the benefits of each. Although helpful, this did not result in a solution. It was getting late, so Mother recommended I go to bed and sleep on it.

The next morning she was in the kitchen preparing breakfast. She asked how I'd slept and then asked if I had arrived at a decision. I said I had chosen the uniform, and the choice was much easier than I had originally thought. My paper route could survive with my old bike, but scouting was something special. It had greater value. Some of my most memorable moments had occurred in scouting. The things I had learned and the friends I had made, were priceless. Scouting was an adventure, while a bicycle was just transportation. My commitment to the uniform symbolized my basic priorities and interests.

I thanked Mother for helping and asked what her choice would have been. She also chose the uniform. When I asked why, she smiled and said, "For all the same reasons."

Mother would also say that in business a product's value is in the eyes of the beholder, and if the beholder (the customer) isn't in agreement with your perception of what a product is worth, then you need to find out why. After acknowledging the customer's point of view, you must set about trying to broaden their understanding of why the price is what it is. Not always an easy task, but if skillfully handled it can bring positive results. This process is best illustrated through an incident I fondly recall as, "Oil And Water Can Sometimes Mix."

While working on assignments in Paris, I often strolled up and down the Seine River observing the artists and artisans practicing their vocations. On one occasion I witnessed—along with another passerby I assumed to be an American—a memorable performance. A watercolor artist working with incredible speed, dexterity and skill was creating a realistic rendition of Notre Dame Cathedral, which was directly across from where we stood. As we watched this genius at work, I felt little doubt that the gentleman beside me was from the southwestern part of the United States. He was tall, lean and handsome, approximately fifty years of age. His clothes were right out of the annals of the old West. Their quality and style gave the impression he must have been successful in either oil or ranching.

Our proximity and mutual interest dictated that we speak. I asked what he thought of the painting but received no response. Perhaps he was too absorbed in what he was observing. But I could hear him muttering, and as his words grew in volume and intensity, I was able to detect what sounded like, "Ain't he the best dawg-gone somethin' you ever did see!" Although it was asked rhetorically, I saw it as an opportunity to try again to strike up a conversation. I said, "It certainly is!" Apparently surprised by the unanticipated response, he turned and curiously looked at me. "Oh, ye . . . ahh, do you like him too?" The ice had been broken.

patient and polite tone, "Do ya' wanna know why I paid five hundred dollars for just two hours of work?"

Value is ultimately based upon each individual's perceptions and expectations. The ability to influence others is in large part determined by how well we accurately identify these factors. In addition, a natural evolution takes place in each of us as we grow older. What may have had little value in our youth may later in our lives become greatly important. And finally, some values are more priceless than any work of art. They are the personal beliefs and principles by which we judge ourselves, and are ultimately judged.

LOYALTY

Mother always said, "Robert, . . .
*. . . a loyal person is someone you can count on
because they know they can count on you."*

W HEN MOTHER'S EMPLOYER, Morris
Chamovitz, spoke of her, he would always mention her
commitment and loyalty. He'd say, "I've never had a
more loyal employee." In my early teens, I assumed it
meant someone who is hardworking and trusted. One
day I asked what loyalty meant to him. He replied that
he didn't have an easy or quick answer. He then asked
what I thought it meant. Based on my limited
experience, I replied that loyalty results when two
people respect and support one another. He said that
was a big part of it, but there is much more. Just as he
was about to tell me what that "much more" was, we
were interrupted, and the discussion was never finished.

It wasn't until years later that the subject would once again arise, this time with Mother. One day she and I were having lunch and I began telling her about the problem a particular client was having (as he put it) teaching his employees loyalty. It seems he had hired a behavioral-science consulting firm to assess the relative level of loyalty and make recommendations for improving it. Mother shook her head and said, "Well, the first thing he did wrong was to hire a firm, and the second was to assume loyalty can be programmed into people." At that moment I was reminded of the question I had asked Morris so many years ago. I recounted the conversation and asked mother if she would care to try and express his feelings. After all, he had been her mentor, and they shared similar beliefs.

She began with her own motivations: "Although I felt a deep sense of obligation," she said, "and appreciation for his having hired me, I also knew that his action wasn't out of sympathy. It was based upon a sound business decision. We both gained something in the exchange. No, my loyalty to him developed out of the daily events, both personal and business-related, that I was confronted with. Loyalty isn't created through a written policy or direct order, and you don't instigate situations to test or promote it either. It's something that is developed over time and must be earned."

"Loyalty begins with the business and personal

philosophy of management and the employees, and the closer those beliefs, the greater the chance of developing the foundation for loyalty. The most important ones for me were having an opportunity to work, being judged fairly and rewarded for my efforts, and gaining an education from someone I respected and enjoyed."

"Loyalty also has a lot to do with the human sensitivity demonstrated by management toward workers. For example, when your father was ill, Morris was always offering assistance. Although my pride would never let me accept his charity, I never forgot his sincere thoughtfulness. He also had a sixth sense when something was wrong, and when it was appropriate to offer advice or help, he would. But that's just one side of the story. The other side has nothing to do with money or bonuses; it was the respect he showed me in every situation. Whether it was in front of an irate customer or in management meetings with his partner and staff, I was considered an equal. In fact, he would often say, 'Dolly (Morris' nickname for Mother), titles just tell you what people do. They don't tell you how much of a contribution they are making or how devoted they are.' "

Another factor she mentioned was education. She had never graduated from high school, so he took it upon himself to tutor her and help her become an astute and professional businesswoman. He once told her, "Dolly, you always had the right ingredients to succeed; I just happened to be the one to offer a recipe, but never forget, it was you, and you alone, that baked the cake." She said she appreciated the comment, but she told him no one can do it alone, and even if they could, they shouldn't. It's the sharing that makes it so special.

When it came to her career, she was promoted according to her performance, not years of service. Her ability as a businesswoman, manager and confidant was something of an anomaly in her day. Gender was never an issue with Morris. He would often say, "The only true way of measuring the differences in people is how well they perform; other than that I only see another human being." When it came to Mother, he would say, "Whatever goals I set for the stores she managed, I could always count on two things: she would work her best to achieve them, and she usually did. She was the best I ever had, and her fellow workers were the first to admit it.

She distinguished herself for over thirty years. During that time she was frequently courted by shoe manufacturers and competitors. She rarely gave them more than passing consideration because she knew their offers were only financially motivated. One time I said, "What's wrong with that?" She said nothing, but thinking about it, I realized that had she gone on, she would have said, "What good is a little more money if you don't like where you work and the people you are with? No other company would have taken the time and effort and shown the support Morris did for me." Her commitment and loyalty were rewarded when she was honored for thirty years of excellent performance before a packed house of dignitaries, friends and family.

She was recognized not only for her unparalleled performance over the years, but for her loyalty to her employer and the manufacturers with whom she had built a close personal and business relationship based on mutual respect and friendship. The recognition she received reflected the admiration others had for her more than her outstanding accomplishments. She received dozens of letters and phone calls from customers, manufacturers, competitors and lifelong friends. And to this day, she still receives calls and letters from customers and business associates. This fact alone serves as an on-going testimonial. She would often say to me, "Business events come and go, but relationships are the true measure of success and happiness in life."

My question had finally been answered, including the reason Morris couldn't offer a simple definition. The development of loyalty depends upon the way that companies define their basic philosophy and word their mission statements and integrate them into their organizations. If they attempt to create loyalty by decree, I doubt if it will ever be more than a section in the policy manual; however, if the philosophy is practiced on a daily basis, the mission statement will become a living document, not a symbolic representation of intent.

Several days later I visited my forlorn *loyalty* client. We exchanged the standard amenities, but it wasn't long before the loyalty issue came up. I asked if he minded answering a few questions. My queries centered around the longevity of his employees; their attitude when they entered the company and when they left; the relationship between upper and front-line management and lower level employees; the types and nature of discussions held during the normal course of the workday; how much management knew about the employees, beyond their resumes and work performance; and, finally, the kind of company events promoting relationship-building that would be positively received and well attended. In each case his answers at best were: "I'm not quite sure."

At that point he asked what I'd suggest. What type of retainer would I need to fix the problem, and how long would it take? I replied that my schedule was overloaded at the time, but even if I were available, I didn't think I would be the answer. He gave me a puzzled look and said, "Then what *is* the answer." I paused for a long moment and then said, "I'd like to figuratively introduce you to two people I've grown to know quite well in my life. The first is my mother, and the second was her employer." His expression alone served as his response. It said, "You've got to be kidding, but so what's five minutes? Let the kid talk."

I did and he listened. I left and he acted.

He called several weeks later and said, "I want to take your mother to lunch." I asked, "Why?" He said, "Out of gratitude. It worked." I quipped tongue-in-cheek, "Hey, wait a minute, I was the one who told you the story!" He replied, "You're right, but your mother was the one who 'wrote' it. Should I reward the author or the messenger?" I said, "Well, you know the messenger is usually shot." He paused, and ended with, "So consider yourself lucky!"

In fact, writing this book has made me my mother's messenger. It has been an honor and a pleasure to have shared these experiences with you, but I can truly say the greatest honor has been the privilege of being my mother's son.

EPILOGUE

As I CONCLUDE this first installment of sharing Mother's lessons with you, I am inclined to ask myself what I've learned from having revisited these experiences.

• First, that no one person holds the only set of keys to opening the doors of life's infinite mysteries and endless challenges. For it is the cumulative knowledge passed down from generation to generation that has secured, and will continue to ensure, the perpetuation of our species.

• Second, that everyone and everything on this Earth has a purpose, value and place in the natural order. When we begin to disrupt that order, even in the smallest way, the whole will ultimately suffer.

• Third, that it is critical to step on the Moon and look back at our Earth, to avoid losing sight of the bigger purpose and meaning of life.

• Fourth, to respect all things and all peoples, not just out of an externally imposed moral obligation, but also from an internally directed ethical one as well. Understanding this can only enhance growth, maturity and success, not hinder them.

• Fifth, to trust the basic nature of humankind to avoid becoming cynical and jaded as we confront life's daily trials.

• Sixth, not to take ourselves too seriously, for in the final analysis, we are but a nanosecond in universal time.

And finally, not to forget the true meaning and priceless value of family, friends and relationships. For happiness and success were never meant to be experienced alone, but to be shared. Wisdom and hope reside within each of us, but we occasionally need to reflect upon and give thanks to those special individuals who have contributed to placing it there.

ACKNOWLEDGEMENTS

I WOULD LIKE TO ACKNOWLEDGE the following individuals for their support, understanding and encouragement throughout my life and during this effort.

• *The Popovich clan:* Theodore, Dorothy, Dr. Charles, Lynn, Dejan and Stevan for their patience, love, understanding and constant source of inspiration. Uncle Montgomery, Aunt Kay, Cousins Teddy and Melanie Popovich for providing a model of dedication to education and commitment to family.

• *The MASR Team:* Manly Applegate, Catherine McGurren, Dennis Ciccone, Joseph Doskocil and Jim Stuchel who helped make this dream become a reality.

Tom and Julie McKenzie for their sensitivity, guidance and commitment to excellence in education and friendship.

• *The Editor:* Ms. Nora Deakin Davis for her genius and belief in this project.

• *The Graphics:* Paul Grabhorn, friend, colleague and final impetus to "*take the high road.*"

• *The European colleagues:* Ingrid Osswald for her years of support, love and guidance; Tom Kirkwood for his lifelong friendship; Dr. Herb Levine and Sonya Luck for sharing themselves and the city of Berlin. Ingrid Gardner-Stefan for her boundless energy and enthusiasm. And special thanks to my colleagues and friends in England, France and Italy.

• *The Special supporters:* Dewey and Jean Vanich for their love and support; Vana Nespor for her constant "ear"; Steve Zinram for his constant support; Ms. Charlotte M. Bacon for the formative years and Tom Gaydos for the later years. Patricia Blackburn Hudson for our childhood and future experiences. *The Core Team:* Bill Robertson, Jim Waddell, Bill Shaw, Jane Mergler, Martie Nauseda, Sharon Nelson, Major Bruce Berwick and Crystal Campbell for sharing their minds and their hearts. *The White House Global Conference Team:* Dr. Robert Corell, Dr. Franmarie Keel, Dr. Nancy Maynard, Tom Harvey, Dr. Ahmed Meer, Misty Church,

ACKNOWLEDGEMENTS

John Elkind and Richard Lukens for their commitment
to country and the global environment.

- *In Loving Memory of:* Morris Chamovitz.

Mother always said, "Robert . . . *success was
never meant to be experienced alone, but to be shared."*